FIRST CITIES

Marilyn Hacker

FIRST
CITIES

COLLECTED EARLY POEMS

1960–1979

W. W. NORTON & COMPANY
New York • London

For information about permission to reproduce selections from this book,
write to Permissions, W. W. Norton & Company, Inc.,
500 Fifth Avenue, New York, NY 10110

Manufacturing by The Courier Companies, Inc.
Production manager: Amanda Morrison

Library of Congress Cataloging-in-Publication Data

Hacker, Marilyn, 1942–
First cities : collected early poems, 1960–1979 / by Marilyn Hacker.
p. cm.
Includes index.
Contents: Presentation piece—Separations—Taking notice.
ISBN 0-393-32432-X (pbk.)
II. Hacker, Marilyn, 1942– Presentation piece. II. Hacker, Marilyn, 1942–
Separations. III. Hacker, Marilyn, 1942– Taking notice. IV. Title.

PS3558.A28A6 2003
811'.54—dc21   2002044869

W. W. Norton & Company, Inc., 500 Fifth Avenue, New York, N.Y. 10110
www.wwnorton.com

W. W. Norton & Company Ltd., Castle House
75/76 Wells Street, London W1T 3QT

1 2 3 4 5 6 7 8 9 0

For Iva

And in memory of
Russell FitzGerald
and William McNeill

Contents

The poems in this book, with the exception of fifteen omitted pages, poems that seemed too slight or too self-indulgent for reprise, comprise the text of my first three collections of poetry, published in 1974, 1976, and 1980. *Separations*, the middle volume, contained poems written before, as well as after and simultaneously to, the poems of *Presentation Piece*. Specifically, the poems "The Terrible Children," "Jeremy Bentham in Guanajuato." "Señora P.," "The Song of Liadan," and the sequence "Prism and Lens" were written between 1958 and 1962, and, as the work of a poet under twenty, might be classed as juvenilia, along with "Chanson de l'enfant prodige" and "An Alexandrite Pendant for My Mother" from the earlier book.

I have chosen to respect the young woman who wrote these poems by not making any revisions in the text, except for the correction of typographical, grammatical, or spelling errors that had passed into the original books.

—MARILYN HACKER
November 2002

PRESENTATION
PIECE

Part One

Presentation Piece

About the skull of the beloved, filled
with unlikely innocence, liver pâté,
tidbits in aspic. You were never
anybody's "lover," should live
in staterooms full of temporary homage.
The corridor slants, cradled on the
crest of an
earthquake. Far above, smokestacks
proceed through badlands of snapped bridges.

About the skull of the beloved, filled
with a perilous remedy, sloshing
into the corners of the damp eyes
where you are reflected, twice, upside
down. The last image before
death is recorded photographically
on the retina for half an hour.
Prints can be made. The darkroom
is at the end of the corridor.

"These are worlds that were his thighs." You are
the assistant purser, translating
and filing telegraphic messages. "Arriving
Thursday 2 PM." "Take another little
piece of my heart now baby." "Armed and awaiting
signal before tides change." One of the messages
may be for you. "In an affluent society
cannibalism
is a sexual predilection."

That is not fresh meat. It was kept overnight
in a tub of brine. Hand remembers
the ribs' wet parting, the heavy pulse on the palm.
This is not the door to the engine room
though a pulse whines in the walls.
Green velvet ropes enlace a green
velvet chaise-longue, beneath
the purple jewels of the parvenu
empress. Meet me tonight under your tongue.

There is no easy way up. Bite
on your lip; do you taste what I do?
A gold skewer
pierces and joins his hands; the handle
is a five-leafed rose. Let me live
in your mouth; I know a place
where the earlobe is imperfectly joined to the skull.
At sunrise
we can look across the wasted sea for miles.

Learning Distances
for William McNeill

I

Snapdragons in a sandy teapot,
green pepper mottled vermilion
in a fluted white dish.
A film of distances over the yellow-gray
morning. The houseplants murmur. The cat sleeps.
Set on wood, the artifacts of friendship order time.
So much stops in the window.
Leaves etched on light. Who are these trees?
                                    My mother
grew marigolds rimming the retaining wall,
spindly, hard, bright.
                        The trees soak morning
with a smell of alarm and cut leaves.

This is as real as any other language:
your jawbone buttressed by your hand,
a mouth falling to speech through gravity,
the stretch between the corners of my eyes.
Words through wires are
bitter between tongue and palate,
between thumb and forefinger,
abrasion of an undrawn chart.

I could tell you, change moves in the moment.
I could tell you, plant grass in your open palm.
I could tell you, take the chains of a white room,
sit in the prison of a windowpane,
close your hands on pebbled granite hours.
This is as real as any other language.

II

It is a privilege to learn a language,
a journey into the immediate
morning, leaf yellow
filtering the white sill,
shaping the building outside,
the place of human wonder in a structure,
the living figure in the windowpane,
the invocation of the possible
moment demanding this motion:
perception,
placement,
praise.

Each time it is necessary
to relearn the entire
process, not to remember but
re-enter the wrench
of seconds on contracted
muscles, the foam tingling
capillaries, that pulse
beating that vision
on the turn of the light-shot
river, below the double height
mahogany lintel, under the ecru
stucco spilling dawn.

I crushed privet leaves
for the green sap and bitter smell
and learned on broken weeds
the pain of fire and water
which is as real as any other
language.

Chanson de l'enfant prodige

The child of wonder looks in bed
at naked ceilings overhead.
Infinity eats up the skies
as burning teardrops cauterize
his wet white eyes.

The child of wonder cannot pass
the curved rococo looking-glass.
Suspended in between the pair,
body and image frozen there,
he whirls to stare.

The child of wonder, deep in his
gut, knows how long forever is,
and, like a haunted anarchist,
hears a repeated order hissed
not to exist.

The child of wonder juggles word
and number; he has often heard
that theorem is not destroyed
and song, peculiarly employed,
endures a void.

The child of wonder lies alone
and touch or thought ignites the bone
and thrills the flesh. But through the grate
he hears the wind come, insensate,
to annihilate.

The child of wonder watches day
arrive. Premature dawn is gray
and flat upon the wet earth he
perceives intangibility
and is not free.

An Alexandrite Pendant for My Mother

I am not in my country, and my home
shifts in the prism of a purple stone
looped round by slender golden straits. Within,
a fist of windy palm-swards clashes, bends
behind the gray ephemera of rain.
Another night. Dogs bark against the dawn.

The traveler awakens before dawn,
yawns, and shakes off a troubled dream of home.
The stray dogs in the street shake off the rain,
shelter themselves behind a jutting stone,
under a porch; the rooted conscience bends,
evades the drenching distances within.

A window lights, ochers the court. Within,
the shadow of a schoolgirl greets the dawn
with drowsy knees and elbows. Then she bends
and draws the shade, a child's ferocious home
closed round her like a carapace of stone,
rejecting ripe and rot into the rain.

This city is emprismed in the rain.
Echoes rise with morning from within
the courtyard, walled with tile and porous stone;
the maids, kneeling at zinc washtubs since dawn,
sing of men riding, women kept at home
vigilant where the mountain roadway bends.

Vigilant as exile, now I bend
over the mirror of blue tiles and rain
whose silence is the only lasting home,
having no voice to call the streets with. In
another city, nightwalkers watch dawn
break blue on river wharf and pavingstone.

This is an island city, propped on stone,
whose roots are swamp, whose tallest tower bends
when trembling earth shatters to a new dawn;
as when, across the lake, glimpsed through the rain,
serpent and eagle coupled signs within
the glyph of death where warriors make their home.

Mother of exiles, home of enduring stone
within the glimpsed point where the road bends,
rain fortune on my voyaging this dawn.

The Dark Twin

                  turning in the brain, to wake
with wires behind his eyes, forking the joints
akimbo. He wakes, wired,
forked fingers crackling, gagging on his tongue.
We wake, turning.
                  Spined against the floor,
his spine turning, chest hollowed,
air in the wires, sparks
glinting from the wired ceiling, tapping
his sparking fingernails. Coughs, cries.
The dark twin doubles on the floor, swallows his tongue.
Splashed to the dark pole circuited behind
the eyes, the dark twin snaps his spine free, slaps
his palms against the ceiling. Charged beads fly.
The ceiling, polarized, batters his cheek with metal.
Tears free skin. Tears ribs,
torn pectorals off metal curved away
black, behind the cracks, dried,
that are his torn lips. More.
Buttocks and shoulderblades grind on the floor
gritty and green with brine.
                  They wake.
We wake, turning.
                He, gargling blood, turns,
born, on the wet floor.
The dark twin turns in the brain. We wake.

From *The Old Reliable*

We draw inland for the winter. Skies
are cannonmetal with a smell of snow.
Through the bar the mohair fairies go
with rum-and-cokes and big cosmetic flies.
A young Italian cop sits near the door
smudging his record-book with woolen sleeves.
He turns and scowls when anybody leaves.
It isn't too effective any more.
Over brandy and between the queens
chilled poets plan fantastic magazines
while trapezoidal Margie at the bar
intuits profit on the way things are
and lifts a steaming glass of Russian tea
to winter outcasts on her property.

Exiles

Her brown falcon perches above the sink
as steaming water forks over my hands.
Below the wrists they shrivel and turn pink.
I am in exile in my own land.

Her half-grown cats scuffle across the floor
trailing a slime of blood from where they fed.
I lock the door. They claw under the door.
I am in exile in my own bed.

Her spotted mongrel, bristling with red mange,
sleeps on the threshold of the Third Street bar
where I drink brandy as the couples change.
I am in exile where my neighbors are.

On the pavement, cans of ashes burn.
Her green lizard scuttles from the light
around torn cardboard charred to glowing fern.
I am in exile in my own sight.

Her blond child sits on the stoop when I
come back at night. Cold hands, blue lids; we both
need sleep. She tells me she is going to die.
I am in exile in my own youth.

Lady of distances, this fire, this water,
this earth make sanctuary where I stand.
Call off your animals and your blond daughter.
I am in exile in my own hands.

She Bitches about Boys

To live on charm, one must be courteous.
To live on others' love, one must be lovable.
Some get away with murder being beautiful.

Girls love a sick child or a healthy animal.
A man who's both itches them like an incubus,
but I, for one, have had a bellyful

of giving reassurances and obvious
advice with scrambled eggs and cereal;
then bad debts, broken dates, and lecherous

onanistic dreams of estival
nights when some high-strung, well-hung, penurious
boy, not knowing what he'd get, could be more generous.

The Navigators

I

Between us on our wide bed we cuddle an incubus
whom we have filled with voyages. We wake
more apart than before, with open hands.
Your stomach and my head begin to ache.
We cannot work. You are in pain. I cry.
Outside the dirty window, in the damp
film of new spring, muddy brown children dabble
cardboard in puddles, chalk across a wall
where two boys on a fire-escape eat oranges.
Love, longing makes us both anonymous,
middle-aged, quarrelsome, ridiculous.
You hurt for want of tears. I cry for pain.

Real, grimy and exiled, he
eludes us.
I would show him books and bridges,
and make a language we could all speak.

No blond fantasy
Mother has sent to plague us in the spring,
he has his own bad dreams, needs work, gets drunk,
maybe would not have chosen to be beautiful.

Because we held him while he screamed or threw up,
were good in bed, or good for a hot meal,
we were not given his life by the scruff of its neck
or even the right to speak too much out of turn.
Love, my love, is not what you have done
but what you are just now doing.

Oh, I would hold his head and feed him oranges
to taste his warm home,
pink shrimp to taste the green lick of the sea.
To taste the road, tart, cold wild apples
and long pale grapes with dusty moon skins.
To taste my love, amber Greek honey
that coats his tongue with sweet thinking of bitter.
To taste my love, raw meat, radishes, lemons
and salt rubbing his lips where they are broken.

     II
I spread his callused hand like a closed plant.
Machines and ropes ripped scars across his palm
leaving it tough and skillful. Watching him wake
or read or take my camera apart,
I learn what learning is and how the eye
reverses image into memory.
Have I learned his face in this much time,
grotesque with concentration, creased with sleep,
the fear that grays his eyes at a knocked door,
the angle of his chin when he is lying?
Levi'd, blond and greasestained, the American Dream
cannot love the Jew's devious daughter.
He shrugs her spells off adolescent shoulders.
She cannot witch him with her ancient language
or scraps of denim sleeve under her pillow,
or comb his name in her long hair with ivory.
He never knows whose son he is, and she
would not be other than her Mother's daughter.
Still, for a short while, we shed our myths
like spring skins and sat across a table,
over dark wood laboriously translated
till we, precarious, unique and human,

with naked hands and eyes, spoke to each other,
and something freer than necessity
tangled our arms and backs, merged our blue mornings.

III

You made an algebra: his tastes in food,
when the dinner guests would be too much
for him to keep his poise, his surly moods;
to calculate how often you could touch
the real boy like your dream sharing our bed,
one arm sprawled off the mattress near your head.
He slept. Your hands relaxed around his chest,
and all the ambiguities could rest
between your shoulder and his shoulderblades.
I saw you move your mouth against his nape,
wanting to wake him in your arms, afraid
of how his face would age coming awake.

IV

His Wife at Bellevue

Trackless and lost between piss-colored walls,
she huddles on the bench arm, hides her face,
shakes with sobs or dry retching. The intern calls
names in a bored voice. People shift in place.
Clocks sweep toward morning and she hides her face.
Between the red felt collar and her hair,
her neck is cracked with white beneath the brown.
I draw an old man. Three boys turn to stare
over their bench to see what I have down;
one has a bloody gash beneath his hair.
I am a stranger whom she cannot trust.
She hid her face and let me bring her here.

My hand quiets her trembling. Since she must
feel some hand on her sickness and her fear,
my hand is on her shoulder; we are here.

       V
Across the mud flats and the wide roads, over rivers and
       borders,
by bus, truck, trailer, car and foot,
my two loves have gone, the dark and the fair.
Truck drivers, salesmen, schoolgirls on vacation
taste the salt fruit of their bodies.
They breathe strange air; strange hands press their
       shoulders,
strange voices speak to them.
Mother of exiles, save them from wind and rage.
Mother of journeys, let the sea be kind to them.

Along the highway, despair and dead animals
steam on the macadam. Sheet-white, the sky
closes them in. Miles apart, in a mud-wide state,
they sing out loud, and the long road is empty
from red hill to scrub-bush. Branches are bare with heat
and it's only May. Home and the ports
swing like a compass-needle, both far away.
Mother of exiles, save them from wind and rage.
Mother of journeys, let the sea be kind to them.

Together, briefly, they sit on splintered pilings.
Thick, spit-yellow foam slaps the Diesel hulls.
Storms are in the Gulf; the catch is north.
North on an old coast, landlocked on my island
dry in soot-thick summer, I spin their warmth.
I loop their names in words. One road is closed

to women and conspirators. I plot. I sing.
Mother of exiles, save them from wind and rage.
Mother of journeys, let the sea be kind to them.

    VI

When you told me that he was in jail
again, I scrounged two hundred for his bail
in two hours, wired it down, came home, threw up,
cried while you brewed me coffee, and threw up,
and threw up every thirty minutes flat
for two days, till the airline ended that
and flew him back. Pale, tired, clean,
I took the Carey bus at two-fifteen
and waited at the terminal for him.
He had new, checked, pegged slacks. They'd cropped his
      hair.
He said he was surprised that I was there
and had I dieted to get so thin.
He asked why you weren't there, and I said, well,
you were engaging in diplomacy
and would be waiting up at the hotel;
which meant, you had to wait around and see
his wife. We took the bus back. It was dark
inside, but floodlit girders looped the park.
Grained, heavy cones of light spilled on the sky
as planes dropped to their runways through the mist.
There was a groan of engines as we kissed
and searchlights limned my hand over his thigh.

Seventy-Second Street; so tired it hurt.
The florid Slav bursting his dirty shirt
could see from the cash window what we were,
a trio of unluggaged travelers

wanting cheap beds and anonymity.
You signed for two, although he could see three.
Two bulldykes teased an acrid teenage whore
pinioned with dexies to the lobby door
and wondered if distinction could be made
among us, who was trick and who was trade.

The walls were hotel green. Someone had drawn
blue crayon mountains facing the iron bed.
We shelved our change of underwear. I yawned.
A swish of cars, a whiff of the dried dead
came through the blinded courtyard to the halls.
You went away that night. The tangled sheets
were heaped and ribboned underneath our feet.
I held him combed in foreign sounds. Thin walls
enclose nocturnal lexicons. He dreamed
of walls, baked concrete glaring at the sun.
Thick sewage sucked his chest. A milky gleam
slid on the trustee's buttons, and the gun-
barrel cocked on his hip swelled twice its size.
(I ground my fists in pillows, reading him.)
He threw his hands up to protect his eyes
and woke knocking his elbow on my chin.

VII

Bailed out too soon, back in our den of exiles,
he dreams of ships and speaks to us in code.
He hides his golden back from the June sun,
learns music from you, teaches me prisoners' games,
reads novels about glorious escapes.
Freedom is fugue, and love is a disease
the way they teach blond boys in Gulf port towns.
He is too sullen and too beautiful.

Deafened by music and his longing silence,
my mouth and hands no longer speak for me.
Writing, my fingers brush, and rub on him.
Talking, my tongue hits salt, and tastes him.
Then, where he was, an empty space and dreams,
the clean sea and his naked body, gold
in a spray of sun, round hard arms sweat oiled
reaching to fold me in. Between his hands
I wake; we, loving him, new strangers, wake.

VIII

A knot of journeys underneath my ribs
bursts like coming when an oilboat prow
slices the river night southward to sea
while humpbacked tugs chug north with open doors
between the hawsepipe flushing and the stalk
where two lights flash for barges. I will go
north on the coastal shuttle to the Keys
or southwest, over the border, across the mesas
down the devious flanks of red clay mountains
to the plaza lights of another city.
Amidst these exiles, I on my own ground
am exiled. I know the joy of journeys,
drowsing through dawn on a humming bus
rushing northeast, someone asleep on my shoulder;
woke with the palms of leaves pressed on the windows
in a coastal forest, smelling the sea;
crossed foreign mountains in a stranger's car
fleeing the unbelievable police
on the same ocean, thousands of miles south.
Distance is sometimes bitter in my mouth
but always spiced with something to be sought
or seen ahead, the sea again, the green

of ancient stone, old trees on a new sky,
the gaslight of a plaza, Spanish tile
chilling my bare feet, spiced tripe on my tongue
with onions in the morning.
This round exuberance could conquer art.
The air spins with adventures, and I spring
on my new body, letting them reach me
and catching open-handed. Air recoils
beneath my soles. Blue sky, scarred concrete
are walls to bounce off, grips to stretch and reach.
I hit the ground like live waves on a beach.

IX

My old city sinks to river winter.
Immobile and alone, I learn to lie
at desks, drink brandy, know my age,
digest somebody's overwritten page,
and love can't turn my stomach any more.
I vomited some bile, and I survive
with guts gone rational to stay alive.
Say if my hands are fit for making charts
that have been idle in their older arts.
Winter and age; we three are in our harbors
trying to make a basin of the sea
to bathe our hands together in, all three
sharing water over depths and miles
and losing touch in distance, speech in style.

X

Orpheus and animus,
drawing back to journeys now,
leaving me on shores behind
streets and shutters of the mind

as a new October streaks
dry hollows underneath our cheeks:
All that I have learned from you,
all that I have failed to learn,
I will order up again
with an overcautious pen,
making models, giving names
(nothing ever stays the same),
initiate the change that moves
the peripheries of love.

Part Two

Concordances

for Joanne Kyger

I

Although I draw the philodendron
its leaves yellow and die; although
I draw the fringy coleus
it drops branches in first-freeze tantrums.
My walls are covered with growing plants
that died of cold and parasites.
So that isn't what it's for.

II

"The transverse beams that hold the snow," he said,
"darken the women's long days with eaved shadows,"
aware, amidst these rocks, that architecture
breathes in elemental lives.
Invent the house around a court, invent the women
gossiping over the well-shaft, invent
the novel again.
Even the weight of a quartz-veined
garden stone in a closed palm
dropped to thigh height, lifted
to eye level, jerked back and thrown
blueprints machines in the mind.
We are creatures of structure.

III

It drops through levity and aspirations:
pun with a landscape drawn around it.
Can you define a bottle with your elbows
and why try? (wanting to pull it off
more than anything.) "That is *not*

one of *my* attributes." Disguised
as a long girl eating peanut butter sandwiches,
winding her calves around the chair legs, she leans
forward, the gap of her black V-neck revealing
the rowed dugs of Ephesian Diana,
spurting equations and wine.

IV

A man and a boy in a dirt lot
adjoining the construction site,
the man in blue clothes like a uniform,
the boy, a pale child on a brown block,
in shorts and gray knee socks: they talk.
The wood fence screens them from the street.
The man rolls up his sleeves and hauls
a pick up from a pile, heaves at the ground,
the fence, then spares the fence. The boy sits on his jacket,
white knees folded against the dark.
Dusk connects them, blotting street and tools.

A man and a woman in a green room
across the street from the lot, sitting
at a small mahogany table, placed
behind a row of potted plants,
begonia, philodendron, lemon shrub,
watch the man talk to the boy.
Over a bowl of greengages and figs
smoke hangs on the visible wind.
Between pictures of other rooms, light filters west.

Cities

for Link

Wrapped in thick sweaters in the high cold room,
we lie, holding each other, on my bed
covered with drapes, saying the names of cities.
The tree in the yard is heavy with snow,
the house is still as a boat in morning,
and I taste Alexandria on your tongue.
You traveled on the bodies of your lovers
away from the madwoman with keys
who locked you in her bedroom.
Smashing a vase and a tray, hiding the knives,
purchased no passport from the humid walls
soaking up voices shrill with loss. Soiled organdy
covered windows out over a city
where they spoke one language under the trees
and mauve skies opening evening.
There was a word like a lozenge on your tongue
and words buzzing the height of the darkening room.
How old were you the first morning,
awake in nervous freedom in a stranger's bed,
thinking of monsoon rivers, sheeted snow
blowing over the domes of possible cities?
Now you have visited many cities.
You draw their figured maps over my tongue.
There, mannered wolves track children through the snow.
There, the outlaw poet in his room
looks from the rumpled table to the bed
stained by the glimmer of a backward morning.

But there was another map you hid with the knives
in the buzzing room, and all your clever lovers
will never find the key.

For Elektra

My father dies again in dreams, a twin.
She stands above his dying like a small
vulture in curlers, twisting her veined hands,
knowing he died before. Looselimbed in underwear,
he slips from indolence to agony
on a rumpled double bed. His round
face flattens with pain. I, overgrown,
watch and fall distant till the dark green wall
is tentative beneath my palm. I fill the window light.
He is my father and my father's twin,
dying again. She did not kill or save him
with her dry hands. She does not touch him now.
The screech of her nails on my cheek. I presume
too much in giving you my mother monster
rehashed in pincurls from a guilty dream
where she slaps my hand for taking cakes and cocks
on my plate and failing, failing.
I will speak to you. You are not my brother,
unmasked on the river path as I long for exile.
Those black figures on the snow, too simply
dark fingers on a white thigh, establish
the clean hierarchic myth.
                          Brothers and brothers
pass under, pass over, but I never had
a brother. Lustful shorthaired virgin
bitch borrows the voice and says,
"Your Mother is my mother. Dare."
How she bores me with her metaphors.
I would rather make love and poems than kill
my mother. "So would I. Have you done
flaunting your cunt and your pen in her face

when she's not looking? High above your bed,
like a lamppost with eyes, stern as a pay toilet,
she stands, waiting to be told off
and tolled out." Waiting to be told off,
Miss Bitch puts me to work for nothing
at being my own brother, with such sisters.

The King of Cups Reversed

The King of Cups reversed has agate eyes
looking away and a stern chin.
He empties out wealth and suggests
the Army for a year, construction gangs,
a handbook of calligraphy: hard change.
Cold cash sticks to the ribs. No more
boys before breakfast. Clean your plate;
eat what the cats won't. In the midst
of opulence, he indicates the light
of one lantern on a windy crag,
brooding where the Fool fell or flew away.

His colors are yellow and blue. His boots
track up and down on the ceiling. This
is a way to break through. The poem
is about itself, breaks on its lines
and curves over them. We used the cards
to comment, and they sang the Tarot Blues
from tacky triumph to four swords turned down.
Real death is an ordinary card,
a low number in the virile suit.
It doesn't turn up often
                              like the pain
of cold bright afternoons when swords
are the three walls of a heart with no door.
March is a bad month for archers. The King
is hoisted on the horns of goats and bulls
as the sun nudges the cards to balance.
Reversed, the King of Cups suspects he's mad,
which knocks determination on the chin

too square and long. He has had
houses on the cliff over the tossed sea
where circling birds whistled like blades.
Now on this fidgety island, he
hands out silks and portents, telling the same
visionary tale of hills and rivers
in the dubious traffic of the bay,
while fishy elegance shakes for the eyes
of damp beasts and the winged ape hidden in the tree.

Ruptured Friendships,
or,
The High Cost of Keys

I am obliged to repossess
some nooks and crannies of my soul.
I do not think of you the less.

Tonight's ragout would be a mess
without the red clay casserole
I am obliged to repossess.

The green chair suits my dinner dress.
The silk throw makes a pretty stole. . . .
I do not think of you the less.

Six forks, two serving-spoons, and, yes,
a platter and a salad-bowl
I am obliged to repossess.

Indeed, I say, more courtliness
would land me quickly on the dole.
I do not think of you the less.

Malicious mischief? I confess
the quicker I forget that role
and do not think of you, the less
I am obliged to repossess.

Elektra on Third Avenue

for Link

At six, when April chills our hands and feet
walking downtown, we stop at Clancy's Bar
or Bickford's, where the part-time hustlers are,
scoffing between the mailroom and the street.
Old pensioners appraise them while they eat,
and so do we, debating half in jest
which piece of hasty pudding we'd like best.
I know you know I think your mouth is sweet
as anything exhibited for sale,
fresh coffee cake or boys fresh out of jail,
which tender hint of incest brings me near
to ordering more coffee or more beer.
The homebound crowd provides more youth to cruise.
We nurse our cups, nudge knees, and pick and choose.

Lines on the Death of Madame de Staël

When she lay, dropsical, myopic, dying,
exiled from Paris, harried across France,
they realized at last that she was trying
for something more than getting in their pants.
That old-boys' club of desultory lovers,
toothy and shrill, gathered around the bed
and watched the bloated aspic under covers,
with the carnivorous despotic head
carved down by loss of teeth and hair in fever
to a hooked relic of the Fisher King,
hawk order with an epigram, deliver
last cutting justice. The cathedral ring
reverberated from the walls, intact,
while strained and astigmatic eyes still looked
caroming after the last artifacts
of reign, that one mute boy, that one loud book.

Alba: August

One morning you woke me
kissing my shoulders
as the rooster on the next block crowed.
New light
blued in the window full of plants,
and the next-door crash pad
got Sergeant Pepper in the day's first groove.

Dancing
between moving limbs,
the slow flowers
of our friction opened
together. So quickly
you were salt and sweet
on my tongue, like the desert
we drove through, asleep
on each other's shoulders.

Alba: October

Falling asleep or waking
my mouth is full of brine
like the taste of your skin.
You are in
another city, climbing
a hill that views the sea. Under
the fat light of bay
windows, shiny omnivorous
leaves crunch open for a wet
lunch. Born
in a city without
seasons, you walk
into the room.

Part Three

Aquatic Park: 1967

This is the dead poet's academy
at five o'clock. Here comes the fog. Two winos
and a curly long-haired kid
have scrap fires going on the sand. A fat
Italian sitting on the *Chronicle*
on the sparse grass turns up
his transistor radio to hear
the baseball scores. I
never met him. He named
you, you brought me here; his ghost
is what we leave on the littered slope, watching
the digestion of the bay, watching
the drunk poets come back. Bringing
brandy.
                              Seagulls
                              circle
                              Long
                              Pier.

One nurses the
brandy while his boy
friend does cartwheels. They
want to be taken to dinner. We
can't afford it. They
try being ebullient. We
really can't afford it. They
stay in the graying park, one
squatting on the grass with the bottle
between his knees, the other
standing on his hands. We
go off rail-balancing, leaving
the brandy, into our
biographical information.

Iceplants: Army Beach

Your body glistens like a new
subway token, nipples the color of copper
turned out of the light. You
ring true skimming the sea, splashing
and pulling me after. Your
wet shoulders incite me to spurious literature
while jeweled ice spatters my belly and thighs.
The black thatch
at your crotch sparkles;
your cock shrivels. We are standing still. We dare
each other in, stung numb
by sea-foam.
Like jumping off a wall I wouldn't
try I ran
into the cold sea up to my eyes and fell
off a sand-bar. Behind me
you grabbed my hand and pulled
me to my feet, drawing
me back in that clasp
to the shore.
Our hands are the same size.

To say
I fell asleep on the beach
and woke
to see your narrow hips blocking the sky:
a lie. Past driftwood,
at the cracks the tide slapped on the shore,
you stood against a flag of sand and sky,
etched dark on the sea.

Behind the cliffs iceplants clutch the dunes
to shape. We face embankments of cement
with dynamited doors. From catacombs
under fake hills, an army watched the sea.
We stagger through a passage in the dark,
around a corner, toward a gap of light,
a two-foot hole. We crouch and clamber out.
Here were gun emplacements. On the walls
around the rift, chalked, SURFERS SUCK DICK
JOHNNY AND MICKI. And the shifting hills
held with rooted tongues of red and green.
Below, the city falls away
white on slopes under the seamist.
There is a poem in touching
or not touching. The poem
defines the tension between skin and skin,
increasing, decreasing, rhythmically
changing the space it defines.
This puts us on the edge of the cliff
crunching iceplants underfoot. Between
camouflaged gun-turrets, two boys cruise
each other. How much of the poem
is about touching or not
touching? Fifty feet below
in the glint of waves through mist, a naked man
with a wristwatch and a walking-stick
approaches, but will not reach,
two horses spurred through the foam.

The Art of the Novel
for Bill Brodecky

The afternoon breaks from a pale
morning on the water of maps
hanging above the desk. Cities
interest him more than people. Geography
is a kind of vast gossip. I always
gossip in poems, mostly about myself,
hinting at inadmissible longings.
I want Everything. Every day
this week I woke up so happy
I felt guilty; warm legs
wrapped around mine. I can't
stay in this beautiful city forever.

I am inventing a city
in these lines. The people
are half real, living
in my correspondent city, created
for them with streets and buildings,
trees and the necessary harbor.
They frequent a bar and perhaps a beach, but I
take them from one place to the other.
You can draw an accurate map and say:
This is where *she* lives with her young German
from Buenos Aires. Five blocks away
in a converted carriage house with a back garden
lives an older painter who covets them both,
usually confusing love and politics.

It is almost always a spring morning. Will I ever
start to work early? We remember the pale

profile out of Goethe. He can't
make his head a compass, disparages maps
and gets seasick on Green St. I have land legs
now, imagining a network of double cities
from here to Leningrad. I might be happy
writing novels, if I could color into geography
like the plate of fruit I painted yesterday.
It is almost always
a spring morning, in the air a longing
to confuse myself.

Before the War

We are asleep under mirrors. What do I
look like? Your mouth
opens on a dream of altered landscapes.
Hidden in the Iron Mountains,
the adolescent general is in love
with you. Noon light stands in the window,
cloudy and white. They are using mustard gas.
That night child anarchists besieged the corners.
Tin cans exploded in front of us; rhythm
escaped in the blistered rain. Everyone
was hungry. You sound
like that in the morning, someone
told her on the telephone, and all
the bar heard it Friday night.
Culled from a garden in Pacific Heights,
the charred corpse of her last lover, ankles crossed
at a vulnerable and tender angle,
embellishes the service porch
above an architecture of dead boys.
It happens every morning at the gas
station while we are still asleep
around the pillow like a third lover.
Covered in burning Saran Wrap,
the young attendant knocks the telephone
off the hook, crashes through
the plate-glass window
and flames out like a screaming Bunsen burner
under the open hood of a '39
Renault sedan. I wake up with your elbow
under my neck. Come here.
Tell me what that eruption on the sun
is.

Landscape for Insurrection

While they drank themselves into a fog,
we planned: Could we survive in the hills?
They stood in the embrasure of the bay
window. I thought of the long climb.
Those uniforms! black brocade on a red ground
and leather hipboots scored with stars.

This is a transformation. Daystars
are crumbling on the rocks above the fog
as damp hands score my shoulders to the ground.
I am out of breath. In a valley between hills
there is a walled town. Mornings we will climb
the rocks to count tankers entering the bay;

I'll seed a plot with spices, dill and bay
and chervil. Now the slopes are spiced with stars.
Light corners the next rise that we climb.
Prickly grasses part, releasing fog
that wreaths around the leveling of the hills
and humps up the slopes close to the ground.

Winded again, I only ground
my teeth and kept going. Dogs began to bay
from the valley at the disappearing hills.
The swollen moon and punctured stars
dangle above the hilltops and the fog
that swallows our long shadows as we climb

and spits them back into the valley. "Climb
up here a minute! What are these tracks on the ground?"
Instead, we sit on a rock, watching fog
track up from the ocean highway and the bay.
"I used to know the names of all the stars."
"Funny, nobody ever named these hills."

In a wrecked lean-to on the highest hill
we hide our things, and smoke outside. Lights climb
up from the bridge, planes pass between the stars.
We rake a pile of stuff left on the ground:
shoe, cartridge, paper, keeping bugs at bay
with cigarette smoke curling into fog.

Covered by fog, we will come down from the hills
into the dark towns on the bay. To find us, you must climb
to this cleared high ground, marked with flares like stars.

The Sea Coming Indoors

The war is far away, sweet
birdsong around the villas on the cliff.
Breakers crash below the dining room
where a gawky Filipino girl
rearranges and rearranges
silver forks on a white linen cloth.
I have given her
your skin, but your mouth
curves around a secret. Speak.
Tapping the salad forks
on her thin left wrist, she paces
the length of the window; a yard away
the drop behind glass
turns her stomach, and a vision
recurs: she is climbing down
the cliff in a gold dress, loose rocks
and thorn bushes bite her palms, these new
shoes will slip, little slides
of dirt and pebbles brush her ankles.
         You
will not come back, decked
with garnets and thorn bushes, hefting
a live grenade. When
you take off your shirt, I see
a line of tiny rubies set
in the central furrow of your chest.
See, my hands are empty. I close
my eyes and forget what I am holding
You are not here. Gem grains
crease my palm. I am looking at you.

Salt air wreaths the door as it opens.
A gap flickers in skin. Elegant
insects twitch to life
in rock shells on the slope. She huddles
on a ledge, unfolding
like a kite before herself unfolding
her hands. It is too late. The seeds
of her disease cling to her wet palms
at the edges of vision. I am sitting
in front of the window, counting
silverware. I have given her
your skin.

Attack on the Iron Coast

The trees are waiting. Three
brown horses, ridden by
twelve-year-old girls with long
brown hair, shoulder each other
at the tide's edge. This
ocean was always
heartbreaking. The rocks
are waiting. Wedged
in a sandy shelf halfway
up the cliff, full of buried
shells and sand-dollars, two people
are waiting. The sun
is an incandescent
solid. On top of the cliff,
in front of the billowed
barbed wire, banging the backs
of their bare calves on the rock-face,
four people are
waiting. The tar road
west of the lake, leading
between the hidden bunkers to the dwarf
pine grove, is empty. A motorcycle
lies on its side on crushed
iceplants next to the road. Inside
the buried passage to the fort, broken
cinder blocks and fused
sandbags frame the still
city beyond the trees east of the lake,
glowing blue and gold. Blue-white
with darkening maroon strokes, naked

to the waist, a man sprawls
on the broken rocks. His skin
is blue-white, the knife slashes
maroon. Flies hover in the clean air, waiting.

Pornographic Poem

You are walking
down the corridor. A man
in striped boxer shorts comes
out closing the last door. It is
the bathroom. Not really
the last door; the corridor
turns there. Your room
is beyond the turn. The third
door on the left. A blond
boy with long hair in faded
jeans and no shirt walks out of the
bathroom, turns. The man
passes you as the boy turns; he
has a crew cut. You are sweating,
your feet are damp in old sandals.
There are no windows in the corridor;
it is underground. Below it
is another corridor, and below
that. Above it
is another corridor. You think
of the window in your room. You can
have a window because of the
hill. At night, if you are
alone, you explore
levels you have not yet seen, under
the DC bulbs. Sometimes
you pass a person on the dark stairs, but
usually not. Barefoot
on the faded figured rug, you can
stop in front of a closed door, hear

a saucepan clank on a hotplate, skin
sliding in sheets, somebody
swallowing, coughing. You always
save the last level for next time. Old men
stay on the upper
levels. A tanned
young man with curly black hair
goes into the bathroom. You
slow down. You go into
the bathroom.

Forage Sestina

This is for your body hidden in words
moving through a crumbling structure.
Between heaps of plaster, chicken-wire
snaggles the gaping floor. Stripped of beams,
cement encloses more cement. A wall
mounds up between parlor and dining-room.

Explicit shadows grapple through the room
which is a ruined city. Falling words
erode veined gullies in the nearer wall.
This is to see if only structure
communicates. Under a beam
an outlet spouts tongues of stripped wire

and your breath crackles like a shorted wire.
You are standing behind me, even in this room
which is a camouflage. Signal beams
flash through the casement, and our words
cadence them, shushed with light, making a structure
of light and sound bouncing off the bare wall.

I want to touch you, but you are the wall
crumbling, the report over the wire
service that there were no survivors. Structure
demands that we remain inside the room,
that you cannot be hedged in easy words
like skin or hands, that we cannot look through the beams

of the burnt roof and see stars. All the beams
were hauled off. Concrete floor, ceiling, walls
surround us. There is one window. Words
cannot be trusted. Capillaries wire
swiveling eyes. If we search this room
we may be able to plot out the structure

of the whole building. We were told that the structure
is flawed, that the searchlight beam
from the bridge pierces cracks. If the room
begins to rotate, floor becoming wall
et cetera, and white sparks dribble from torn wires,
there has been a rebellion of words.

Words will peel off you, revealing the structure
of a human body branched with wires. Over the last beam
keeping the sky from the walls, vines drip into the room.

Part Four

Imaginary Translation I
for Gerald L. Fabian

These foothills shelter me from war and love.
The pig-boy doesn't trouble my sleep, nor does
his sister, slinging pears in a wicker basket.
That orchard rolls below my garden
where I spent this morning pruning
the rose-of-Sharon bushes I transplanted
from the pasture above Agate Cove.
Once a week the post comes from the city:
Joseph, my redhead cousin with the nose,
has joined the Army. Lifkin's second book
was mentioned twice at Madame G's soirée.
And R has made acquaintance with an actress.
(Dear R, it is less painful now to think of
your eyes, and your abominable French.)
This afternoon I walked up in the hills
along the coast. Gorse-bush and choke-robin
and robber's-purse were all in bloom.
I caught a tan lizard and let him go
and watched three butter-colored butterflies
converge over a whitened dog-turd.
Along the skin-hued strip of beach below,
a scraggly green platoon down from the fort
was firing ragged rounds into the tide.

Imaginary Translation II

Those men and boys who are
your week-end lovers, I wish
them affluence and patience
to charm you and to learn from you
and teach
you by reflection how you move;
and that woman who turns
open-eyed in your arms in your green room
as pine boughs crackle at the city fog,
I wish
her a long sojourn in a summer country
with someone faithful, blond and tall,
gentle and exigent
and not you.

Imaginary Translation III
for Bill Brodecky and for Tom Disch

There was no reason to stay in that city
any longer. I had concluded my affairs
well enough. I knew no one but colleagues,
and the foggy season
was starting. That last night, fortified with brandy,
I took a late walk on the waterfront.
Boats lowed; the triple-masted shadows
of long-beached ironclads striped the streets.
Next to a bar I'd heard of was the theater.
You know the plot, how the traveler,
too rich or too poor, goes to a foreign theater
and, from front row center, or the rear balcony,
sees that the star, or the last one in the chorus,
is that person, touched and held perhaps three days,
but loved (the traveler knows now) all these years.
It was not three days, but three years
we were lovers, and barely one apart,
with a few thousand intervening miles.
But there was the name on a list of names.
And the ticket window was open. I went in.
The loge was obviously best. Much leather
and brocade; faces I would not
recognize under elaborate hair,
feathers and smoke and lace. Many seats
were empty. I could imagine, seated
in the dusty maroon cut-velvet
armchair—you know the story. Then
they milled onstage, shrilling a language
not the one the audience was chattering
and neither of them mine. Footlights swallowed

sweet hashish and contraband tobacco:
a whiteflossed creature, breasts like apricots,
pelted as St. Sebastian. When the arrows
whistled—those gold wounds were not real,
but they bled. *Shoot first who loves me best.*
The archer had green-scaled metallic breasts,
green shoes, green flower headdress, a blond beard
and silver eyes. I did not think, "What monster
have you become?"—only tried to find
those brown arms and attenuated thighs
in the rush of particoloured limbs.
"There," as somebody in fuchsia satin
tossed back black hair; but was it you or I
who pushed their hair out of their eyes like that?
And those were certainly the wrong ankles
on the blackfaced dancer. The laugh
was right. And the singing voice,
if you had ever learned to sing. You would
have had those eyes, if you had blue eyes.
Perhaps it was three days and not three years
I knew you, and your language was my second
language; perhaps your lover lived
in another city, and your copper
hair covered your forehead as we danced.
But we grew up in the country with the same
foster-parents, always suspecting
our mother was the same, until we first
laid damp palms on each other.
The footlights dimmed; some of them clumped
to sing, while spotlit dancers cruised the aisles
accosting those whose income or whose gender
was too plain. I was safe in the loge
from scented satin thrown over my face

pushed into pungent ambiguities
in which I tasted you. The story ends
with the pilgrim discovered and embraced
by the stellar lover, with the voyager
carrying off the aging *rat de ballet*
or sneaking away unrecognized: "Who *is*
that person? Surely someone I know?"
I walked out through the incense and liqueurs
with everyone who did not stay. The fuchsia
satin (whose hair was kinkier than yours),
the blackface, the albino Cupidon,
the naked skull, the rouged and bearded diva
lounged to coffee and brandy at a bar.
I looked at them. They looked at me. I walked
out, towards home, in the sequined fog
of this city, which is, by now, mine.

To the Reader

Pacing from room to room trimming the plants,
I walk heavily on my heels. I smoke
foul-smelling French cigarettes. Invoke
that portly bluestocking in gardening pants.
Won't do. And if Catullus learns to cook
while Lesbia goes to the bars to cruise,
you haven't put up anything to lose
except two hours to read a different book.
Boys will be boys and wonder in their rooms
if fame could be a sociable disease.
"I'll sleep alone and murder whom I please
and find another lover when the moon's
in Scorpio." Be grateful to our Mom.
She let you off with cancer and the bomb.

Nightsong

A plant will draw back vision to its source
and crack the glass if it is very tall
to grow by moonlight whose sufficient force
prevents my eyes from banging on the wall.
There is an undulant red satin back
that, exoskeletally ribbed in gold,
incites the digits' giggling maniac
to hold to have to hold to have to hold
to have cold water thicken on his tongue
until his anal gravy binds the sky
while no one looks particularly young
and certainly not you, friend bone, nor I.
Although you sweat and pant and show your skull
and tease your hair with overheated birds,
it's not my fault that you are beautiful
as a refrigerator full of words.
I was a polyglotted acrobat
who hoofed on a technicians' tour of hell,
but now I'm going to drop the alphabet
and stay at home and teach my wound to spell.
And if you think my singing voice is nice
and want to comb my hair and think I'm sane,
I'll cool my ears by sucking on some ice
and let you borrow someone else's brain.

The Muses

C'est Vénus toute entière à sa proie attachée . . .
—RACINE, Phèdre

Don't think I haven't noticed you
waiting in the other room to kill me.
She came too close to the root, my sister,
rooting in the coals for a pristine
death, wishing, oh, wishing
it wasn't so flabby,
the skin creases gone livid and all
those sensual surfaces puckering
like a plucked chicken
(and that was what she
  thought of seeing a
  limp cock for the
  first time: a
  turkey neck).
Now I stand in front of the
oven, warming
my hands. At my desk
after sundown, my nails turn blue.
And you are waiting in
one of the other
rooms. Sometimes you are a
middle-aged woman, your skin
flabby, bluish, your hair
frizzed out in filaments, picking up
whispers of plots to Do You In
you can almost hear. You pat your face
feeling the puckers and creases, knowing
it is already Too Late, even
if it is only Tuesday, when you dreamed
it was Friday.

Sometimes
you are a Beautiful Boy, out of a
pederast's fantasy, dark-curled
golden and edible, mouth
curved in a snarl or a lie. Rage
wrinkles your cheeks in a newborn's imperative howl
and to placate you, I can only say Yes
I will curl my hair, lend you twenty dollars, Yes
the world is ending, fashion is all, if
I were honest I would starve myself to death.

And one of you
will tear out chunks of my hair, and one
of you will slap me across the eyes, and
one of you will hit my head with a rock
at the top of the stairs and
one of you will kick me in the stomach
and one of you will smash at my nails
with a lead paperweight. O lying
at the foot of the stairs, my legs
wedged against the door, fingers
sticky against my eyelids, listening
to you tear up the rest of the house, I
will not be convinced
by your onyx
identical eyes.

Waiting

I get up every day before the mail
and go through the same matinal ritual:
piss, wash, make coffee, warm my hands,
prune and water my three rooms of plants,
feed the cats, answer yesterday's letters.
Something frightening is going to happen.

But nothing extraordinary will happen
today. There's no interesting mail:
a postcard, bills, very professional letters
that only want a kind of ritual
reply. I chew my pen and watch the plants
and would like very much to put my hands

in dirt or in someone else's hands.
I don't know what it is I want to happen.
I think that I am safe behind the plants.
There was no coded message in the mail
today. "You have let your part of the ritual
lapse. We are informed by certain letters

the key to the kabbalistic letters
has fallen into uninitiate hands.
Purify yourself with the first ritual
cleansing. We may not say what will happen
and cannot contact you except by mail.
Beware of interceptions and of plants."

I wish I lived alone with growing plants.
I wish I had a lover instead of letters
from strangers. The arrival of the mail
is the only time that someone hands
me movement. Nothing real is going to happen
yet, except this desiccated ritual.

Later, I preserve my wit in ritual
dissection. The cats sleep in the plants.
The fog burns off toward evening. If I happen
to say: impatience and despair, in letters
to strangers, I am putting myself in their hands.
Dismissals and evictions come by mail.

Mail this now. Then I will tell you the ritual.
Rub your hands with leaves from these three plants.
Wait for their letters. Tell me what happens.

Like Aschenbach in Arizona

My two companions are tireless, and the landscape
makes the human form irrelevant
except as a naked surreal intrusion.
Still, I remember you. Yesterday,
we walked through the Petrified Forest.
Between foothills of striated clay,
logs turn to semi-precious stone;
molecule by molecule, crystal
pervades the wood. After an hour, our bodies
were covered with fine white alkaloid dust.
The sky was bluer than your eyes. The process
continues. Cerebral crenellations
crunched under our feet. I could imagine
parts of your body grown massive,
translucent, severed, defined. Bloodstone
searing the veins. "I'm not your bloody Muse,"
you said, and indeed you aren't.
"But I will be." Well, here you are,
a jet trail above the highway,
preceding us to California.
I'll never see you again. When I came back
from scrabbling toward the sky up a bleached mound,
Tom was examining a quartz block
blotched with agate and amethyst. "If the light
never changed, I'd go mad in an hour."
We talked about drugs and poetry. The sky
is bluer than your eyes. I am using you. The process
continues. The hills heaved in the sun.
It is harder than the stoned mind imagines
to sink into a landscape. The dust will not

accept you. The stones will not accept you.
There is not enough time between breaths
to feel the crystalloid osmosis
begin. My heartbeat calls me back,
the pounding in my ears, the sweat
sliding down my ribs. And here I am,
a small, redheaded, pungent woman, not
your bloody Muse. Today
the three of us climbed down into the Grand Canyon
about a mile, after our hangovers.
The sun seeped into me like orange juice.
Swifts sliced the clean air.
I interpose a figure, charged
with repercussive energy, imposing
human-scale on a landscape.
Charles posed Tom and me on the lip of the gorge
for tourist shots. This piece of petrified wood
in my hand is hot and smooth
rust-mottled milk with crinkled apertures
I stick my fingers in. Tonight, we'll be in Las Vegas.

Part Five

Sestina

for D.G.B.

For a week now our bodies have whispered
together, telling each other secrets
you and I would keep. Their language,
harder and more tender than this, wakes
us suddenly in the half-dawn, tangled
dragons on their map. They have a plan.

We are stranded travelers who plan
to ditch our bags and walk. The hill wind whispers
danger and rain. We are going different ways. That tangled
thornbush is where the road forks. The secrets
we told on the station bench to keep awake
were lies. I suspect from your choice of language

that you are not speaking your native language.
You will not know about the city plan
tattooed behind my knee. But the skin wakes
up in humming networks, audibly whispers
over the dead wind. Everybody's secrets
jam the wires. Syllables get tangled

with bus tickets and matchbooks. You tangled
my hair in your fingers and language
split like a black fig. I suck the secrets
off your skin. This isn't in the plan,
the subcutaneous transmitter whispers.
Be circumspect. What sort of person wakes

up twice in a wrecked car? And we wake
in wary seconds of each other, tangled
damply together. Your cock whispers
inside my thigh that there is language
without memory. Your fingers plan
wet symphonies in my garrulous secret

places. There is nothing secret
in people crying at weddings and singing at wakes;
and when you pack a duffelbag and plan
on the gratuitous, you will still tangle
purpose and habit, more baggage, more language.
It is not accidental what they whisper.

Our bodies whispered under the sheet. Their secret
language will not elude us when we wake
into the tangled light without a plan.

Villanelle
for D.G.B.

Every day our bodies separate,
exploded torn and dazed.
Not understanding what we celebrate

we grope through languages and hesitate
and touch each other, speechless and amazed;
and every day our bodies separate

us farther from our planned, deliberate
ironic lives. I am afraid, disphased,
not understanding what we celebrate

when our fused limbs and lips communicate
the unlettered power we have raised.
Every day our bodies' separate

routines are harder to perpetuate.
In wordless darkness we learn wordless praise,
not understanding what we celebrate;

wake to ourselves, exhausted, in the late
morning as the wind tears off the haze,
not understanding how we celebrate
our bodies. Every day we separate.

Sisterhood

for Dora FitzGerald

No place for a lady, this
back-country gateway comes
up from dreams; the wounds
are an entrance, or a season ticket.
The morning freshness, the
summersend mountain calm:
distractions. "What do you
call this town?"

No man will love you, no
woman be your friend, your
face will go away, your body
betray you. We wrestled
to the floor, his fingers
blanching my elbows, cords
popping his neck. Don't look
into the sun. Don't squint.

He lay on the concrete
ramp of the bus terminal. I
massaged his back and shoulders through his clothes.
I opened his trenchcoat, peeled
its collar away from his thin
white shirt, his thin chest.
Staining the slashed white
yellowish pink, those wounds.

When you give the ghost
bread and water he asks
for, you incur prophecy.

"Why have you come here,
woman? Your city
is far away. We do not speak
your language. Your sister
is dead.

"Take off your rings
at the first gate. At the second,
your crown of lapis lazuli.
You must leave your golden
breastplate at the third, and below
the gallows where he hangs
who forgot you, and will not rise,
break your mother's scepter."

They have killed him
often. He bled
on the concrete floor. My hands
were not healing. They took him
into the next room. I heard
gunshots. I woke screaming.
At the bottom of hell
he swings in the stinking wind. She watches.

We, women, never
trust his returnings. He takes
the bread and water, but
the words on the paper
are illegible. His body
lies severed on the white sand
and the pieces are not
food, they are stones.

We gather those
jewels and wear them,
lapis in the crown, amethysts
over the nipples, garnets
oozing on cool
fingers. The gateway
dreams itself up, and we eye the surly
guard, and strip, and go down.

Elegy

for Janis Joplin

Crying from exile, I
mourn you, dead singer, crooning and palming
your cold cheeks, calling you: You.
A man told me you died; he was
foreign, I felt for the first time, drunk, in his car, my
throat choked: You won't sing for me
now. Later I laughed in the hair between
his shoulder-blades, well enough
loved in a narrow
bed; it was
your Southern Comfort
grin stretching my
mouth. You were in me
all night,

shouting our pain, sucking off
the mike, telling a strong-headed
woman's daily beads to dumb kids
creaming on your high
notes. Some morning at wolf-hour
they'll know.
Stay in my
gut, woman lover I never
touched, tongued, or sang to; stay
in back of my
throat, sandpaper
velvet, Janis, you
overpaid your
dues, damn it, why are you dead?

Cough up your whisky gut
demon, send him home howling
to Texas, to every
fat bristle-chinned
white motel keeper on
Route 66, every half-
Seminole waitress with a
crane's neck, lantern-jawed
truck driver missing a
finger joint, dirt-farmer's
blond boy with asthma and sea dreams,
twenty-one-year-old
mother of three who got far
as Albuquerque once.

Your veins were
highways from
Coca-Cola flatland,
dust and dead
flies crusting the
car window till it rained.
Drive! anywhere
out of here, the
ratty upholstery smelling
of dogpiss and cunt,
bald tires swiveled and
lurched on slicked macadam
skidding the funk in your mouth
to a black woman's tongue.

Faggots and groupies and
meth heads loved you, you
loved bodies and booze

and hard work, and more
than that, fame. On your
left tit was a tattooed
valentine, around your
wrist a tattooed filigree; around
your honeycomb brain webbed
klieg lights and amp circuits screamed
Love Love and the booze-
skag-and-cocaine baby twisted your
box, kicked your
throat and the songs came.

I wanted to write your
blues, Janis, and put my
tongue in your mouth that way.
Lazy and grasping and
treacherous, beautiful
insomniac freaking the ceiling,
the cold smog went slowly blue, the cars
caught up with your heartbeat, maybe you were not
alone, but the ceiling told you
otherwise, and skag said:
You are more famous than anyone
out of West Texas, your hair is a
monument, your voice preserved
in honey, I love you, lie down.

I am in London and
you, more meat than Hollywood
swallowed, in Hollywood, more
meat. You got me through
long nights with your coalscuttle
panic, don't be scared

to scream when it hurts
and oh mother it hurts, tonight
we are twenty-seven, we are
alone, you are dead.

Nimue to Merlin

Who are you anyway? Did it take long
to get here? I don't live in a tower,
but I don't have Thursday salons either.
I take care of my plants. I'm not as young
as I look, and I like to be alone
most of the time. May I fix you a drink?

Shoo off the cat. I usually don't drink
before dinner, but I've had a long
day, working. Are you traveling alone?
I've heard about you. Once, I saw your tower
from the high road, when I was very young
and curious. I'm glad that I'm not either

now. And here you are, which means you've either
changed, or you want something. I wouldn't drink
so fast if I were you. How young
you look. Your skin is like a boy's, and long
hair becomes you. If you stood up, you would tower
over me. Don't you find, when you're alone

long, you lose eyes and voices, let alone
people's tastes and smells. Excuse me, I'll either
embarrass myself or you. In your tower
when it's almost dawn, and you can't drink
or sleep more (I'm presuming) and it's a long
way down, and some idiotic young

bird shrills up, do you think, when you were young,
if you'd let it hurt, let well enough alone,

things would have gotten better before long?
You wouldn't be here now. I don't think so either.
Here's pears and cheese. I'll make another drink.
Your hands are cold. Your neck is stiff as a tower.

It's already late. The road back to the tower
is crowded with political loud young
men with no wives who've had too much to drink.
Do you want to go back there tonight alone?
I won't keep you. I won't chase you, either.
Sometimes the nights here are extremely long.

Lie alongside me. I'll build you a tower
in my hand. You're either too old or too young
to be alone here. Open your mouth. Let me drink.

Rooms in Bloomsbury

The horrors of the personal, revealed
in indiscreetly published *cahiers,*
lean on the pristine chronicle. "Today
A and Z used my room instead. I feel
nothing, although I saw them on the bed
one instant before switching off the light
again. Read Stendhal in the bath all night."
As, circumspectly in that epoch, Z
writes, ". . . then, at last, they published it, and for
the first time public notice shaped my life,
till world events intruded. Even C
could not ignore the change, and, as for me,
I soon displeased my publishers, my wife
and friends, enlisted and endured the War."

Aube Provençale

Absent, this morning
the cock crowed later than the nine o'clock
church bells. Cherry boughs
bronzed outside the casement,
and I woke

sweating, with my hands
between my thighs, from a dream
of archives, wanting you
under me, my breasts hollowed in the arc
below your ribs,

my knees between your knees,
my hands behind your ears, my cheek
furrowed in your chest, tasting
our mingled night-sweat, tasting
your sleep.

I'll make a song
on your neck-cords. Wake up,
bird asleep against my hip-bone,
and crow, it's already
morning.

Crépuscule Provençal

Cursing the Mistral,
the neighbor elbows doorward.
It batters on tiled roofs, whips cascades
across the hill-face. Meet me
near the sea,

I wrote; come to me
through polyglot gossip,
and we'll share mountains, oceans, islands.
November is wind and rain
here. Heavy

persimmons, bloody
on black branches, gleamed in blue
afternoon, clear as a hidden valley.
Lapis beyond the green gorge, the sea spilled
its chalice

of hills. It's a month
since I left you, near water, wet
pebbles in our pockets, I'll write, our cheeks
brushed, salt gusts already
between us.

Dark now, shutters bang
stucco. Later I'll drink
by the fire, and let three tongues of
chatter silence an absence sung
in the wind.

Apologia pro opera sua

It appears that almost all the poets who slighted
the theme of Unrequited Love to say
how more of the land than That Boy or That Lady lay
were poets whom somebody had, in fact, requited.
The eclogue on The Natural Order of Things
and The Imperfectibility of Man
ends with blond wife and prepubescent son
waiting with soup and a snifter in the wings.
While William had his visions, Kate baked bread.
Chester is clever with scores and escargots.
Mary kept the books, and wrote one, too.
From the querulous to the universal "You"
is not an unthinkably long distance to go
when the Muse gets up first and brings you breakfast in bed.

The Osiris Complex

No coastline ever
lost a man like this
desert; the sea makes
definitions. Sky
wrapped his neck, sand
tunneled up his bare
chest, slanting against the wind. Were there
bones, were there rocks
that looked like bones, did
limbs shimmer, severed
at sight's periphery?
His body seemed irrelevant, pain
was not real, nor remembered
palms, his nipples hardening
into the life-line. Sky and white
distances of sand, the wind
mixing them, the line
between them going on
perhaps forever, some interstellar
measurement. "Infinity is the
bogeyman of the precocious
child," she said later.
And he: "Naked
in the hot wind, a wooden
staff in my hand, language
retreated in my forehead,
a milky stone, a blind eye."
Were there birds, were there
watery sand-blooms, were there
polished stones the color of blood and eyes?

Only the ancient
weight, the absence
of metaphor, a visible
reddening behind the lids, the wind
changing everything. The wind did not change anything.
(She came with the
rec squad, in the
first jeep, broad little
burnt face, like those
Cambodian girl commandos, axle grease
up to the elbows.
"Pick up those rocks, pick up
all those damned rocks, get them
into the truck." And to herself, "Why
have you brought me here? Last
at the edge of a cliff, those rocks with the ocean
foaming below in impossible
colors. Why
have you brought me here? This catalogue:
one obsidian
femur, a truncated
jasper calf, onyx
haunch powdered with dried blood. Build
a city, let it cover
the earth, make islands.
Obliterate this landscape.")
Were there, finally,
words, arrowy black
motes on the sky? Even the smooth
stones only rattled in his head, he willed
his limbs away, they didn't
go. A corpse keeps
its scars. Riddled with diamond

grains, wind-striped, stripped, sun-forgotten,
lassitude
weighed on his
pivots; he was
screened from his own
pain, by his own pain.
Heavier, heavier, his
ankles belonged to the sand, his calves took root,
his thighs were hollowed by the wind. Bright
pebbles rattled in the bone cage, sang
him to the rock. Yes, with words.
(She came back, alone, at
nightfall. The soldiers
were asleep, dreaming dark girls
licking salt from their elbows.
She came back, black
as lava, twice as old,
tall, tall and
haggard, too
black to look at, hooded
in her own face. "In these
sockets his eyes
elude me. I cannot
describe how the stones
in my hands become dead
meat, keening to be
born. I am an old, bald
horror, as human as
he was, still hungry.
Why have you brought me here?")
"Why have you brought me here?"
he did not say, questioning
his naked arms, juxtaposed

on all that sand, shifting its
topography, all that flat
dazzling
sky. He knew if he
lay down, something
might, or might not
happen.
He would spin centrifugally
into those pricks of
white light, shaken from the
surface, another
sand-whirl. He would
sweep into those distances.
How dense it was, a place in back of the head
where it all goes on; unnecessary warmth,
too heavy, too bright, eyes
balk at it. It was closed, it would not
let go. He finally
let go, finally
put the khaki shirt and shorts back on,
walked barefoot back to camp through the
cooling sand, holding his shoes.
(She did not
come at all. The rocks cast
ambiguous shadows in the
mellowing light,
uninterrupted. Thousands of miles away,
a ten-year-old, chewing the bedclothes, staring
at the projections of infinite
space on the ceiling, asked
the stranger in the cave behind her
eyes, "Why have you brought me here?")

Untoward Occurrence at
Embassy Poetry Reading

Thank you. Thank you very much. I'm pleased
to be here tonight. I seldom read
to such a varied audience. My poetry
is what it is. Graves, yes, said love, death
and the changing of the seasons
were the unique, the primordial subjects.

I'd like to talk about that. One subjects
oneself to art, not necessarily pleased
to be a colander for myths. It seasons
one to certain subjects. Not all. You can read
or formulate philosophies; your death
is still the kernel of your dawn sweats. Poetry

is interesting to people who write poetry.
Others are involved with other subjects.
Does the Ambassador consider death
on the same scale as you, Corporal? Please
stay seated. I've outreached myself. I read
your discomfort. But tonight the seasons

change. I've watched you, in town for the season,
nod to each other, nod to poetry
represented by me, and my colleagues, who read
to good assemblies; good citizens, good subjects
for gossip. You're the audience. Am I pleased
to frighten you? Yes and no. It scares me to death

to stand up here and talk about real death
while our green guerrillas hurry up the seasons.
They have disarmed the guards by now, I'm pleased
to say. The doors are locked. Great poetry
is not so histrionic, but our subjects
choose us, not otherwise. I will not read

manifestos. Tomorrow, foreigners will read
rumors in newspapers. . . . Oh, sir, your death
would be a tiresome journalistic subject,
so stay still till we're done. This is our season.
The building is surrounded. No more poetry
tonight. We are discussing, you'll be pleased

to know, the terms of your release. Please read
these leaflets. Not poetry. You're bored to death
with politics, but that's the season's subject.

A Christmas Crown

I

Son of the dark solstice descends the tree
into the winter city. Riversedge
receives him as the rusty currents dredge
our frozen offal heavily to sea.
Child of our Mother in the death of light,
torn out of blood onto a shattered mirror,
squall reasonable hungers to our terror;
it will not take so long tomorrow night.
The starry dragon will be drawn to scale,
exhaling central heating on the crib
or carton where the infant graingod breathes
and coughs up stringy gobbets on the wreaths,
decides to live; earth-warmed air swells his ribs
while she smiles at the moon, her plate, her pale.

II

While she smiles at the moon, her plate, her pale
reflection, tideridden ladylove
of corner boys and epileptics, of
remittance princes, alcoholics, frail
dexedrine beauties, we in lust of male
muses had best rededicate
postponed mornings. This time she might not wait.
In her thin arms the child begins to wail,
robust and greedy, sucking every sin
but hope out of her teeming hemisphere.
Will he rebuild our city where we stand
ritually dumfounded by the hand-
reflexes of any infant? Where
will he learn our hunger, and begin?

III

Will he learn our hunger and begin
the politic ascent? Our history
glyphs our bodies; querent to him we
flash autonomic broadcasts. On the skin
of a distracted shopgirl: Monday's news,
produce of Sussex, a sermon on Greed.
I praise you, baby who still cannot read,
accept, acclaim, admonish, or accuse.
I have my woman's winter in my hands;
my mouth bleeds with a homeless appetite;
the several importunities of lust
grease my regard. In solitary trust,
I pledge infidel vigil as the night,
swollen with day-birth, chills, cajoles, commands.

IV

Swollen with day, birth chills, cajoles, commands
simpler directions. We still want to go
back to the Good Place. We could finish grow-
ing up in an orderly, four-seasoned land-
scape, we tell each other, drinking gin-
and-limes on the terrace while the monster flock
moves through the hot rain to the western dock.
Here we are languid adolescents in
fiction, waiting for a Protagonist
to get us moving. Outside, the real snow
drifts to the real street. They've closed the bars,
and whisky voices slide above the cars'
tarry andante, caroling her slow
pains as she brings her belly to the tryst.

V

Pain. As she brings her belly to the tryst,
invalids, children, and insomniacs
turn in their beds, wanting the daylight back;
and lovers, whose replenishment consists
of little sleeps between betraying dreams,
wake, thinking that blue window is another
blue window, and that heavy kiss is Mother's
send-off on a class hike in the Extremes.
More would be only fiction: how the dying,
the pious, the powerful, turn on their own
wheels of year-dark, emerge, or stay behind.
I don't know what the nursling in my mind
will grow to, only question an unknown
quality, voiced with a newborn's crying.

VI

Quality voiced with a newborn's crying,
impotent as an infant to reply
to questions or the chocolate-covered lie:
O wouldn't it be cozy to stop trying,
O give the music-sheets, the cup, the child
back to the nice lady and come *on*
(who on the wet steps to the Underground
in Baker Street turned with jonquils and smiled).
When I have grown accustomed to the cold,
when I have grown accustomed to the dark,
the lean meat and the narrow bed, I will
not have accumulated virtue. Still
drifts feather the entrance to the park.
The birthday is eleven hours old.

VII

The birthday is eleven hours old.
The novelists' two sweet-stained daughters play
Camps under the kitchen stairs. Today,
hardly anything is bought or sold.
Hardly anybody eats alone.
Almost no trains run. Almost-suicides
and almost-murders lie in rows outside
the noisy quondam operating-room
where an exhausted intern, twenty-three
years old, mops up and sews. The children sing
below our gossip. Roast and fruit and wine
and smoke mix in the air near dinnertime.
The guests file foodwards while the darkening
sun of the dark solstice descends the tree.

SEPARATIONS

Geographer

Geographer

for Link (Luther Thomas Cupp), 1947–1974

I

I have nothing to give you but these days,
laying broken stones on your waste, your death.
(The teeth behind kisses.) Nothing rhymes with death.
Richter plays Bach. My baby daughter plays
with a Gauloises pack. Once I learned pain and praise
of that good body, that mouth you curved for death.
Then your teeth clenched. Then you shivered. Seeing
       death.
Another of those mediocre lays.
Little Brother, of all the wastes, the ways
to live a bad movie, work a plot to death.
You worked your myth to death: your real death.
I've put my child to bed. I cannot eat.
This death is on my hands. This meat dead meat.

II

There is a cure for love. It is absence. There is a cure
for grief. (It is absence.) I cannot say,
you died, and I don't want to live today.
I fed my child. I learned to drive a car.
I went to work. The baby is in bed.
This is a formula I used before.
(I ate a veal chop.) Word, word, word: the cure
for hard nights. Somebody was always dead,
but not, certainly, you. You rattled speed-
ing, seven-thirty, through the door,
awash with daffodils. Did I stay
up all night drawing the bowl of fruit? I did.
And then we went to bed and slept till four.
You kept the drawing when I went away.

III

Sorry, I can't make any metaphors.
There is no talking horse. Billy the Kid
did what he did, and he died. Death is no mid-
wife birthing you to myth. You died, that's yours;
death is nobody, death is a word,
dying happens. People die. I will die.
You are dead, after five minutes of dy-
ing. Were you afraid? Last night I heard
of another poet dead, by her own hand
it seems (oh how I wish there were more
boozy women poets, aged sixty-seven:
new book, new man, wit and kitchen noted for
flavor). *If there's a Rock-n-Roll Heaven*
They sure have a Hell of a band.

IV

Metaphor slid in on the radio
like vision's limit; we see the night sky
a planetarium dome; mind, or eye,
won't take starry infinity, won't know
for more than a dawning shudder: I will die.
You died. Once, we walked along the beach
in the Pacific autumn twilight. Reach-
ing for something, knowing you and not knowing, I
asked, were you afraid of dying. "No,
I don't know." I wanted to say how, ly-
ing in bed, I was ten, in the swish of cars
through rain outside, I knew, what you knew, and know
nothing now, that I was going to die,
and howled, hurled into the enormous stars.

V

This is for your body hidden in words
in the real city and the invisible city:
your words, Jack's, Hunce's, Lew's, Gerry's, my words,
golden scarabs, a carapace of words
crystalled opaque over your eyes, this death
that was your eyes. Hating words, I fumble words
into a bridge, a path, a wall. My words
are not to coax your saltiness this time;
they freeze you in this agate slice of time
where you would not be now except for words.
I am thirty-two. I have a child.
You were twenty-six, never a child

never a grown-up. At my feet, my child
puts a box in a bigger box, babbling almost-words.
You were eighteen, a smooth-cheeked, burning child,
black and gold on the snow where terrible chil-
dren honed the facets of the winter city.
I was twenty-three. I let you be the child.
Last century, I would have died in child-
birth, proving nothing at all in my death
except that women were duped, even to death.
I love my loud brave dirty woman-child.
She and I have gotten through, this time.
And you snuffed yourself out at the same time.

Bright in a frieze, the figures whittled of time
rescued from love and money, friends and child:
gem-lit bodies locked under my fur (near time
the Museum closed), we writhed, reflected; the time
we howled and rolled all night, elbows and words
gasping absurd (to get to work on time

we slept, at last, feet to head); the time
we mapped an imaginary city
on your graph pad. Shanghai, Leningrad, what cities
we pored over in picture-books, marking time!
Trite, how a little boy giving the slip to death
skips over maps, and one slip is, anyway, death.

Now I will be face to face with death
which has no face. I have had two weeks' time
to heft and weigh and hold and swallow your death.
I have written a lot of lines that end with *death*.
I have held your death the way I hold my child,
but it has no weight and it has no voice. The death
of a red begonia from frost, the hibernal death
of the Heath horse-chestnuts, colored, odored words
pile up. But I have not found the words
to thread the invisible waste of your death;
the quicksilver veins threading the map of a city,
till the lights all froze out, all over the city.

I am alive, in a grey, large, soft-edged city
you never saw, thinking of your death
in what is an imaginary city
for me. Once, I imagined a city.
You were born there. You took me there. In time
somebody might have thought it was my city.
Night after day after night, I mapped the city
on the brown geography of its child;
and the cliffs and hills and gemmed sky charted the child
like a wound flowering the streets of the city.
The wound clotted with jewels. The jewels were words.
I left you in the city, and took away words.

From the gutted building, we salvaged words,
raced down Nob Hill at midnight, bad child, bad child,
thinking we'd gotten away with it that time.
Past one now, and the night contains your death.
Now you have visited too many cities.

The Terrible Children

The Terrible Children

You, born half smothered in a caul of myth,
whose bursting heart was drowned in waves of sky,
salt-swollen on the scorching sand you lie,
bright flagellant beneath the whip of death.
You, who never tasted the fruit,
who woke wide and immobile in blue fire,
now, stretched to silence on the singing wire,
fall through limed fissures, naked, rigid, mute,
while summer children underneath the tree
gather the thick-dropped apples where they lie.

Hand in hand down snowcrusts, arrow-poised
arm folded under arm, dilated eyes
windows thrown open on a world of ice,
mirrors turned on an onyx checkerboard.
Their faces are not of brothers or lovers.
Blood never etched this congruence of curve;
no tie explains the way symmetric swerve
and flash of sound and movement ape each other,
nor explicates the bent, left-handed grace
their yoked forms sing, striding from place to place.

They fish the streets. A mirror is their net,
distorting human form before their pure
absurdity into caricature.
Politely offering dry hands and wet
smiles, words odorous as white hemp-flowers,
the gesture of a bow; a sudden turn,
they disappear. Against the sky they burn
in silhouette. And through the shrivelled hours
the others tread the inverse of their steps,
laughing, toe to long heel, till laughter stops.

The delicate purgation of a tongue
turned back over purgation: paradox
within a more intriguing paradox
of involuted mouth. The large eyes' long
panes reflect ritual violence
hung in a room apart, the separate
bright strands conglomerating intricate
woven patternings of death and silence.
The geometric flights of music, each
intoning a formality in speech:

If you are angle, I am complement.
If you are circle, I am circumscribed.
If my hands mold, yours is the form described.
Your voice is my familiar instrument.
I sound a note, and you complete the chord.
Your eyes are an inscription in my hand
that reads my face and tells me what I am.
My singing resonates beneath your words.
A move completes a move; as games are played,
if I betray, you are the one betrayed.

Crying ice tears, their faces washed in snow
till clean as knives, they walk through winter, wading
in frozen air. The moon is always fading
above them. Stars in intaglio
imprint a pattern on their upturned brows.
Loosely, their fingers latch. The star-seared mark
glows bloody effulgence in the dark.
Within the scarlet aureole, their mouths
cross, meet and linger, press to rediscover
the treacherous salt pungence of each other.

Jeremy Bentham in Guanajuato

For myself, I would prefer to be alone,
savoring the privacy of my decay.
I cannot see a fraternity of death
beneath or above ground. Those without souls
should stay in solitude, to meditate
soullessly. There is a shame in death
when it is old and shared.
                            They've turned to leather.
Terminal wounds scream knives.
Their mouths are open too, in agony,
or in surprise, but calm now, even screaming.
Note that their genitals are gone. The organs
that formed them living abdicate for death.
You speak of flown souls; note these shriveled loins
that make a better line of demarcation.
Mother and child, soldier and priest, lover and lover,
have lost their stories in the lime museum.
Only, perhaps, a crumpled piece of parchment,
Ana Ramírez, dead in her first childbirth
tacked without ceremony on a belly.
And truly, I could not care less for stories
than for a name for each of the grey skulls
piled in the anteroom. Death has a lesson
for us, but not in tragedies and titles;
and these are here because they are
unpaid-for. Nameless now
they bear the better title of The Dead.
My presence cannot disconcert these objects.
(For such they are, and objects of instruction.
They, like the knife of Plato must be used

to fill a function well.) The end of man
is such. I feel some warped affection for them.
Indeed, I would not join their congregation;
these do not value privacy enough.
Sing in their chorus? No; I would prefer
to be alone
           but why the mould and clay?
Dust soon enough, I'll do, alive or dead,
as I do best and speak as I still can.
We make a better audience than worms.

Señora P.

Having no occupation and no child,
she gambles, and her mangy dogs run wild.
Dark-blown blond hair and party-practiced laugh
comfort and mock her from a photograph.
With charity bazaars, she marks the feasts
of saints, adores old actors and young priests.

The Song of Liadan

Liadan of Corkaguiney was one of the college of twelve bards of eighth-century Ireland, called ollaves. Touring the strongholds of the High Kings with her entourage of apprentices, she met and fell in love with Curithir, another ollave. He implored her to marry him. A son of theirs, he said, would be Ireland's greatest poet. She agreed to meet him after their rounds were finished. Later she had afterthoughts. Could love combine with the austerity of a bard's life? And why a son, and not a daughter? She rejoined Curithir, but only after taking a vow of chastity. He placed himself under the same vow, and the two went to live in the monastery of Saint Cummine. To avoid temptation, they were given the choice of seeing each other without speaking, or speaking through a crack in the wall and never seeing; poets, they chose speech. Liadan died soon after; Curithir went on a pilgrimage to Jerusalem.

I

A leaf in the path, a sere
finger of autumn, dust and a sway of branches,
dust and a rustle of death's muse,
blue and black a mantle under brown hair,
a sky, a wind, a note of the swineherd's song,
a step I did not take, a brown ash-
leaf in the path's dust.

My hair shall turn grey presently.
My hair shall be silver as the shocked moon,
my hair a web and my hands jewelled spiders.
I shall lie silver presently,
my hands leaves in the path, shadow fingers,
ice-caresses down the thighs of trees.
The swineherd flings acorns and apples in the afternoon,
roots and rich fungus in the afternoon,
dead flesh and offal in the afternoon,
devoured, mouldering into evening.

The sunlight etches runes over brocade,
two hands' electric juncture on brocade,
clasped fingers across pewter and brocade.
The swineherd sings. Soon my voice will melt to silver-
gummed webs clinging to the breaker's hand.

                               And I am silver

and barren.
Brocade. Our hands clasped in a truce of gauntlets,
a silence above song. Love would be
a myth of god's death, and my bright betrayal
scarlet and purple as a ceremony.

When I was seventeen, I loved a sailor
with sea-grime caked beneath his fingernails.
He taught me navigation and three tongues.
Later, I loved a scholar who spoke two.
My youth was bitter as a hard green fruit,
still bitter on the bough, and never ripe,
shrinking to dry core over a missed season.
Always, they say, gods have been born of virgins
who bloomed divinity, simplicity,
and warming pride. A child of mine
would eat fire, sing death, still my hands forever
with her uncompromised mortality.

Sing,
poets, girls, children. Unguents and incantations
to soothe the thighs, the lips, the hands, the eyes.
For a moment, dissolution. And the moon
bleeds. And the silver shot with
blood. And myself already scarlet,
falling, alive with imminent dying.

II

(First, the word,
   after the word, the cry,
   after the cry, the song.
   When will we know what we are seeking?)

You have imposed upon me a treaty of silence.
You have sealed my lips' stone with passion.
You have melted the speaking stone with your hand's heat
and your warm mouth is a band on mine.

There is a scream between us I have smothered.
There is a loud song frozen on the cold road.

My love is locked in a room without windows.
My ears are invaded by dissonant bells
sudden in cobbled silence. I cannot speak,
and in my body is a fear like metal.

A pendulum strikes on metal
and in my quick heart is the silence of bound hands.

The coming of spring is insidious and cruel.
The mist pervades my throat as it melted the crystal
my voice was. I am weak, and I much preferred
the hard agreement of our truce of gauntlets.

(Having the choice,
      the belly like a full fruit growing
      to burst and die, the sprung song-seeds
      sailing alive on blue air.)

III

As the pulled root shrieks, as
the struck stone breaks, as
glass at a note-thrust
cracks, as
ice slivers from the sudden shard of spring;
cracked, broken, and slivered, shrieking
under the mad, sharp stars,
I shall dance, beloved,
and sing passion's reason to the blind walls.

> Nightingale, falcon and crow,
> Stand me witness to my vow:
> To be more and less than human,
> Perfect chord and barren woman,
> I will give my own heart's blood
> That my song may be renewed.
> Earth bewail and sky rejoice.
> Die, my body; live, my voice.

O saints that on the green earth trod
O Mary, got with child by God.

Poem for Edwin Dickinson

Painting, I make it harder than it is.
Look for the thing.
Center: interstice made by
her bent arm and belly, hand on thigh
tapered to acute angle, concave arc
of breast on top, behind. Behind is yellow,
blued with noon. The focus is her elbow
which has at least five colors: one is the green
her breast is splashed with;
three purples from her back; blue from the spine
meeting wall and shadows; highlights yellow; down the arm
salmon darker than the dappled thigh.
This bend draws colors. Draw.
See in the bent arm resting straightening thrust.
Shadows on the skin mean bone,
muscle curving the crook to wrap the forearm
crossing her far thigh at a lever's angle
lifting the upper arm, dark with heavy shoulder.
Behind is yellow. Sun and lemon
soften the crease from thigh to belly
and the back slope from waist to hip-bone.
Seeing, I make it simpler than it is.

Catherine

Star-cheeked Catherine has a catherine wheel
exploding on the velvet of her chest,
her smarting ribs pried parting by a spoke
of constellations shooting out on smoke
diagonal to darkness till she reels.
Level-limbed Catherine, child of circumstance,
propels herself into the winter dance
of frozen comets, lifts her head to mark
Orion straddling Fourth Street on the dark,
spanning the gutter with his studded limbs.
Catherine lifts her straining lids and swims
under the dazzled torrent of the sky,
darker than wide and half again as high.

Catherine in Love

Her broad bones and green eyes from the Midi
reflected ocean in an infancy
of chilly longing. Looping wavelets broke
splashing his lips with bitter salt. They woke
in the familiar sunlight of a room
turned inland. Gold around her pupils reeled
into a wall of flame across a field;
his tongue touched lip, met cycles of salt spume.

Catherine Pregnant

Eternal pressure shrinks the finite earth.
The waxing body swells with seeds of death.
The mind demands a measure to its breath
and in its convolutions comprehends
the endlessness in which it is contained,
the change that is its necessary end.
Change is neither merciful nor just.
They say Leonard of Vinci put his trust
in faulty paints: Christ's Supper turned to dust.
Winter dries the grass, freezes the dew.
Age may coin a lion on your brow
and stun my moving fingers with a blow,
while each expanding instant redefines
your face burned in my eyes with living lines.

Catherine Married

Their child was born in March. Early in May
he watched her umber-dappled fingers play
in the north window spilling morning light
to get the prongs of ligament drawn right.

She would not work on canvas or on wood.
Near the mosaic coffee-table stood
a six-foot square of cardboard strung on wire:
farms in a starry valley, all on fire.

He tried to work. She yowled more than the child.
He couldn't teach her if she wouldn't smile.
Through June, her wide hands twisted in her lap.
She always smelled of garlic, or a trap.

Guests came to see his paintings. Everyone
turned to the burning valley. He was gone
most of the afternoons, sometimes all night.
His portrait of her glowed with leafy light.

Meticulously, with a paring knife
he cut the canvas features off his wife.
When he came back from taking down the trash
the cardboard valley strewed the floor with ash.

Equinoctial
for Bill McNeill

After the heavy-eyed boy usurer
reclaimed the prism he had dearly loaned,
scavengers took the carpets and the furs,
the crusted draperies nobody owned.
You packed your drawings in a cardboard roll,
wrapped the framed things in a pillowcase,
leaving the god cracked on the shower wall
whose mad benevolence had kept the place
alive that long.
    Spring hazard raises floods
and runs a roadbed through the kitchen door
where predatory witches track in mud.
Absence is a distance gone before.
Downstairs, the Rocky Mountains and the sea
imbue the air with possibility.

Some of the Boys

Scraggly goatee, Prussian moustache
salute each other with a clash
of steins against percussive noise,
in Sunday coats of clever boys
invoking demons in the zinc
basin of a classroom sink.
Repartee and studded leather
draw the sting of chilly weather.
Amyl nitrite and perfume
close the ceiling on the room.
On the carpet near the fire
silence motivates desire.
If the tapestry behind
the figurines is ill-defined
nothing has to be explained
to a body scarred and stained
by the excess of his own,
bruised, exhausted, and unknown.
Agate stare will not be placed
in a humiliated face,
measures the confining walls
as the onyx figure falls
below the cautious gilded frame.
He must look and see the same
drawn skin, nervous extremities
that the naked stranger sees.

Birmingham

Behind that music happening, they told him
"Never look at your face travelling.
Vision stops change."
The vision of his change: a doped rag
cloying his blind runnelled face
after the black melting from there to here,
purple moss over the glistening
surface of a foreign afternoon.
Measures these distances by tastes
tongued in mouths that speak another language.
Gold hands grope him with questions.
Long waxed rooms, guessed words
luminous on his eyelids. To be fixed
in this motherfucking indecision.
Homesick. Fear and an incipient
hardon. The voluptuous interpreter
breathes before that music, only heard,
and a fat child crawling across yellow kitchen tiles
stops and cries and the shaving mirror
of a few thousand mornings shimmers into tears
along with their tall story and he throws
his hand in front of his face to tear
this last long drunk. And breaks more glass.

September

The umber dowagers of Henry Street
gossip from windows while they rest their feet:
The Jew on East Broadway sells rotten fruit.
Last night the cops busted a prostitute;
broke up a crap game in the hall next door—
woke up the kids at almost half past four.
As taken with the ripened fall of words
against the yard as what they saw or heard,
their voices scoop the sun like beautiful
harsh birds, until the cindered yard is dull
with evening, and the regularities
of grubby men and children home to eat.
Two laminated toucans pepper meat
as sunlight sheaths behind the sumac trees.

After the Revolution

There are different ways of dying without
actually dying. I was nineteen.
So was Milo. Pavel was twenty-two. The square
was hotter than this beach; the no-man's land
between July and October
when anything can happen
                              and nothing does.
They searched me. Nothing. They left me behind.
Every touch threatened; not the way a boy's
skin tingles to be touched.
                              If the gift leaves?
Might as well die.
                    I woke up with that line
and a bad temper. We waited
to see them on those balconies
as if they were girls.
                        I hardly know you:
an approximate age, oiled skin,
stones in the sun. We smelled each other.
Fear, yes. And, then, they had touched me.
So we waited. Are you a journalist?
I hope not. Why does it come down to
language? Pressures of bright air
over that other city; incipient autumn
swelled red and yellow skins. An instrument
incises the rough bark (feel it
signalling in the palm's crutch); thick sap
oozes amber marbled cream, the instant's
crystal, for the cabinet, crammed
with history. There are

unchronicled moments, the plane-tree
knifed on the air in the square court.
The boys waited.
           We waited.
                 Dear friend; I am trying
to organize my expedition towards
the source.
          Every bedizened traveller
retailing gossip in the Market with
chunks of dark amber, angels enamelled on tin,
makes me think I can discover, if not
the actual "lake between three purple mountains"
above the falls, at least some old bachelor
with odd tastes, some witch's brat daughter,
who has been there, or claims it, and will show
(but not sell) a pebble, a dried herb
that smells like copper and quince. . . . If I do not
come back, if I disprove your theory
in a large-circulation periodical
or anything equally tasteless, remember
this note, and the token
I enclose.
        I will not be able
to lunch with you on Saturday.
                 Sincerely,
Dear friend;
           Perhaps you will understand
when I say, I can no longer tolerate
this city. . . . No . . . The two young nuns
whom we watched strolling in the cloister
through the gap in the wall . . . if I said, their gait
seemed peculiar; if I added
the ostensible boy poet lodged

in what was Mother's room has got a pattern
to his intensities . . . I will not be
drawn into events that I cannot
control or understand. These things concern
soldiers, economists, geographers,
but I will not be made historical
by chance. Good-bye. Perhaps you know
more of this than I do, have considered
the possibility of my . . . retreat.
I must miss you on Saturday.
                              Yours faithfully,
Read it back. Tell me what I said.
                              Words.
The body's heavy syllables. Touch me.
Say. Nerves said, You will begin
to finish dying. The children are running away.
They are hiding in the gorse bushes. They
dribble your inner thigh. They are throwing
chocolate wrappers from the balcony.
What are they whispering? Tell me.
                              Milo remembered
a child on the beach, a fox-faced little girl
carving something from driftwood. It was late August,
early evening. He was nineteen. He gave her
half his cheese and two tomatoes. She was carving
an old woman in a shawl. Cheese brine
on her fingers stained the dry wood. Her hair
was cropped against lice, gold stubble on her neck.
I thought of touching her there. It was not
Milo, it was I. The salt still on her mouth.
Pavel had a stolen rifle. Milo
had an American pistol. You are not
a journalist?

I'm almost twelve,
she said. I already have breasts.
I can read French. I read *Madame Bovary*.
If they fire into the crowd, I said. I thought,
Pavel would be a handsome grandfather.
We are playing stupid games. I will kiss you, I said,
but I'll never speak to you again
if you tell anyone.
It flowered
his sweaty shirt-front. He crumpled, quizzically,
into the dazed heat. *"Pavel!"*
They searched me. Nothing. They left me behind.
A red ball sun plumbed the translucent water.
She lay on top of me, her knees
rubbing my trunks, her cotton shirt
damp and gritty on my bare chest. Licked salt
off my lips.
I looked for Milo for three days.
Dear friend;
It was once my language; now I can
barely read it. Even this note
may be written in code.
Yours in haste,
Here comes Pavel with lunch. The children
went crabbing with Milo and Douina. Don't
say anything to Milo . . . his job . . .
you understand. Not
as one might have wished.

The Last Time

Alba: March

Coming home to the white
morning light in my studio. Ten o'clock;
down the block construction workers stop
for coffee, beer, a drop of booze. It's cold;
they trample frozen mud. White
sunlight quivers in my head,
slivers in puddles breaking last night's freeze.
I finger keys in my woolly pocket, holding
a grocery bag striped golden with light.

All around the south windows
plants doze and shiver awake
as a new leaf breaks and uncurls. I unpack
a green enamel pot, black pepper, milk, eggs,
with the light melting my legs, like
that boy's long calves last night,
warm moons on my own
when we had grown drunk with kissing
stretched on slippery cool sheets.
I kissed his eyes, mouth, feet. I kissed his knees,
ate honey from the flower between his thighs
and felt it rise with sap against my tongue.
He was so young. His cheeks, as smooth as mine,
tasted of pears and wine, and that smile
was not for painters. While I held him
it swam above my drowned eyes.
Now I organize papers, inks, pens.
I'll draw the coleus again, its leaves
a curvilinear trap for light.

Living on the Edge

Living on the edge
of a continent on the edge
of an ocean on the edge of a grinding
fault on the edge
of crossed blades, salt water dulling
the edge
      of the land breaking back into the ocean.
On the edge of calling him
by dream diminutives: Boychild,
Little Brother, she wonders, did he ever
mistake her for Mother, mistake her
sullen fits for murderous rage
remembering
the double thrust into
her in-
complete, red jewels
stabbing his eyes and outside
the soldiers have started
singing.
Certainly they distrusted
each other's dreams, when he began laughing
minutes before he woke, when she
struck out the back of her hand as her eyes
opened with tears.
        And the old photograph
she kept on the edge
of a glass tray of turquoise
butterfly wings: he is eleven, she
thirteen, they are both kneeling, he

behind her, grabs
her shoulders, she has one arm across
her ribs under her teacup breasts, the other
reaches between her thighs toward his cock;
her head is turned, their open mouths glued.
The scene freezes. We will replay the scene.
Winds have shaped the small trees into
artificial unities. Outside the park
people are doing real things.
They wake up the landscape. Corridors
of eucalyptus over red-needled ground
arrange themselves around. "They smell
like the first time I slept with a grease monkey
and didn't know if I liked it."
                                    The road
crosses the soccer field
down to the beach. A ruddy businessman
wrestles and races his blond ten-year-old.
The field is filtered green. The children scream.

Somewhere in a Turret

Somewhere in a turret in time,
castled and catacombed in but
still on a tan street that
ends with a blue-and-white gingerbread house,
those rooms are still filled
with our pictures and books. On the sill
our black-and-white cat hums after a fly.
It is getting light. When we come in,
no one will ask you to leave, no one will send me away.

Nobody lives in the present, time
has textures past and future that
tongues taste at, fingers feel for.
The present happens in rooms
I am not in; past rooms
are only momentarily
empty, if I knew how
to turn around, I would cross the threshold smiling.
No one would ask me to leave, no one would send me away.

Don't think I'm trying to ignore the time
I piled my things into a cab and left
a note for you and one for the dinner guests.
Those rooms have new tenants. You and I
may never share a closet or a towel-rack
again. We contrived it. I am still
surprised waking up without you every morning.
But I can't camp out in your house or you in mine.
People would ask me to leave. People would send you away.

Still, I am an optimist. Sometime
we may be sitting, maybe near the ocean
on a cliff, and under the blown spray
get tangled in each other's fingers and hair;
and in that arbitrary future, your mouth
and the sea will taste of each other.
It is so easy to make things happen
like a freeze shot ending a movie
so you don't leave, and I don't go away.

But you know about words. You have had time
to figure out that hardly anyone
came back to bed because of a poem.
Poems praise and protect us from
our lovers. While I write this
I am not having heartburn
about your indifference. We could walk
into any room.
You wouldn't ask me to leave. I wouldn't send you away.

Sonnet

Love drives its rackety blue caravan
right to the edge. The valley lies below,
unseasonable leaves shading the so-
seemly houses from the sun. We can
climb down. Cornflowers push from crevices
and little purple star-blooms with no name
we know. Look up. I didn't think we came
this far. Look down. No, don't. I think there is
a path between those rocks. Steady. Don't hold
my sleeve, you'll trip me. Oh, Jesus, I've turned
my ankle. Let me just sit down. . . .
Predictably, it's dark. No lights go on
below. There is a dull red glow of burn-
ing at the edge. Predictably, it's cold.

Return

Sweet enemy, I can no longer
convince myself desire
is your diffidence, your beauty
is unkind, your excellent
long body scorns me.

You rise to me
without laughter or words,
too quickly beneath you I flower
open to what unknown
army.

Lying beside you I
dreamed I was lying
beside you, you smiled uncovering
my breasts, your hands in my hair, you
said "I love"

and long-haired
children lay on a green hill, we
walked past, journey-grimed, sweaty,
tired, we stretched on the slope
our knuckles touching

and their indolent
bodies rolled into a dance of
feathered serpents, sea blue,
sky blue, blue plumes in crystal
rain

around us. I
wanted to join the
dancers, seeding the sky for their own
pleasure. Girls and boys I'll never
bear you

crystallize
behind my knees, where you
once tasted, "I want to
know all the ways
of giving

you pleasure."
Serpents swallowed the rain,
grass, hill. We trudged a crowded
tropical city street; we had walked
for hours

looking for
your car, a room, some food.
Soldiers pushed past, speaking another language.
A dusty blue bus carried
the children away.

But when we
lay down in the yellow
wooden hotel bed, half-dressed
and thirsty,
we slept

knuckles touching,
washed by the hill-
magic we hadn't made;

first you smoothed my hair
and said

and I woke
beside your silence. Hunger
drew my mouth over you, urgent
and ashamed; companion,
adversary,

did we share
a blessing or elaborate
amusement at the infidelity
of vocabularies shared
by passing strangers?

Imaginary Translation

for James Keilty

These two meet for dinner once a week
in the old city. Middle-aged and grey
with some distinction—one wrote a verse play
that revolutionary students speak
intensely of; the other left archives
of an obscure study for politics,
talks urgency to Ministers and tricks
reason from hotheads—they lead public lives
of private circumspection, and they drink
together Thursdays. Twenty years ago
in a strange port, for two weeks and four days
they were lovers. Or enemies. They clink
snifters, wax quotable near 'Time,' then go
home their discrete and solitary ways.

Suggestions of Travel

At seven-thirty, omne animal
post coitum goes to get the car
repaired. Chastened toward chastity, you are
in an uncombed rush. I shall sleep more. I shall
get up still dripping you. Then a hot soak,
Pears Soap and Norinyl. Catch a noon train
north. Red eyelids and the linen stained.
Neither our mouths nor other quarters spoke
except of habit and chagrin. I'll stay
since I'm still here. August's annealing fires
subsumed on winter coasts. Tonight I'll read
in Manchester. Off then, packed all I need.
I wish we both were more accomplished liars.
I wish it wasn't going to snow today.

Occasional Verses

"Your touch is abrasive. My blood seethes and smarts,"
said Sappho. Said Atthis, "Two pints and some darts."

"Stay," said Gaius, "it's keener than scandal when you—"
"I must go now," said Clodia. "The scandal was true."

"Your breasts are like melons, your mouth like dark plums,"
said Petrarch. Said Laura, "Why can't we be chums?"

"You move like a Phoenix on fire," said John.
"I'm off dancing," said Fanny. "You *do* carry on."

"Your glance is a torrent and I die of thirst,"
said William. Said Maud, "Revolution comes first."

"We're relations as well. . . ." Lytton coaxed Duncan Grant.
"We may *be* them," said Duncan, "but have them we can't."

I mull on poor poets who miffed their affairs
while you kip with the Muses discretely upstairs.

Geode

for D.G.B.

It is
from my landscape, and
is another landscape, a country
we never visited
together. I learned
enough of the language to buy bread,
fish, cheese, and wine. You made
friends with the old doctor, both getting by
with scraps of university German. (A coy
joke about parts of speech.) Brown-legged
children raise dust clouds on the one road.
The car door
was almost too hot to touch, and the seat covers burned.
A lizard flicks in the sand. We stood
breathless in that desert, the fleshy gems
full of light. I laid my flushed cheek
momentarily against your arm,
went on.
Inside the mouth of the cave
the jewels are wounded to speech.
They speak. The stones' wounds sing.
                              The surfaces hide
and surface in mutable light, facets
of smoky brilliance
to mass under a pale, veined column.
Hushed limbs shine
bluish, becoming gemmed,
other. No moisture;
the songs of the broken crystal
are clusters of crystals

that fork, accrete, erode.
                              The shaping
                              is painful, the enunciation
                              painful.
The object
stops, shimmering; struck to view,
it glistens, suggests something hidden,
rooted in cool onyx. Soothe
your forehead on stone. Never
is an adverb denoting time.
Listen. I tried to tell you. When the water
is gone, the crystals
still grow.

La Vie de Château
—*a fiction*

That morning, she crisply snapped a postcard
next to his cup. "I think this is for you,"
she said. *Bugger! How does that girl*
know where I am? "How does that girl know where
you are? Only my husband and the servants
know you've come here." "And the children."

"Is she in correspondence with your *children?*"
"Hardly." He smiled, rereading the postcard,
accepted through a swath of sun the servant's
proffered brioches, and more steamed milk. "*Are* you
going to explain?" Postcards fluttered from nowhere,
like the too-clever fingers of the girl.

It wouldn't do to think about the girl.
"I think that I'll go for a drive with the children
this morning." "I think that you'll go nowhere
until you explain." It was almost a rude postcard.
Well, quite rude. How *did* she know? How could you
explain one to the other? Now the servants

had left. He couldn't accustom himself to servants,
or didn't like to think he could. The girl
who ironed, dark and thin, an arrogant smile you
wanted to decipher . . . His children and her children
shouted in the orchard. He'd sent *her* a postcard,
of course. She hadn't sniffed him out of nowhere

with a very naked man headed for nowhere
running like hell (the older woman servant

sailed the plates off)—a British Museum postcard
of a Greek vase. "Let's forget that wretched girl.
I thought I'd have Françoise take all the children
swimming, and spend the morning alone with you."

"Yes, lovely, I'd like to spend the morning with you."
Blonde and blue air, a morning for getting nowhere.
Already he regretted the drive with the children,
regretted, really, consigning them to servants
on their holiday. Could they forget the girl
by lunch? He might send her another postcard.

"What are you looking at?" "Nothing. White lace. The
          servant's
apron." "I know where we'll go." Grappling the girl
like children in the dark. He'd send a postcard.

Villanelle: Late Summer

I love you and it makes me rather dull
when everyone is voluble and gay.
The conversation hits a certain lull.

I moon, rattled as china in a bull-
shop, wanting to go, wanting to stay.
I love you and it makes me rather dull.

You might think I had cotton in my skull.
And why is one in Staithes and not in Hay?
The conversation hits a certain lull.

You took a fretful, unoriginal
and unrelaxing friend on holiday.
I love you and it makes me rather dull.

A sheepish sky, with puffs of yellow wool,
watches the tide interrogate the bay.
The conversation hits a certain lull.

And I am grimly silent, swollen full
of unsaid things. I certainly can't say
"I love you." And it makes me rather dull.
The conversation hits a certain lull.

Gifts

Here. Between us I've placed a smooth stone,
green-veined, with finger-fissures, and a cracked
blue bowl with three yellow pears, and seven miles
of jagged coves, pebbled and bouldered, the jade sea
drooling and frothing them, one dwarfed tree,
a crooked surviving pine, on a tumbled cliff
lookout point. Hold the stone
in your palm, cold
from morning draughts on the window-sill.
The touched side takes your warmth. The cool
side rubs your lips. Your mouth
is on my hand.

Rhetoric

Friend, then, whatever has become of us
since each for each was the anonymous
stranger whose elusive qualities
as Other in the Dialogue more civilized
poets apostrophise?

Foundered on languages,
discovering each was another whose
perceived uncipherable difference frees
or limits, to get this far, just this far,
we have become precisely what we are.

The Life of a Female Artist Is
Full of Vicissitudes

Goes mad,
frescoes in shit on the walls;
cuddled and spoon-fed for
3 weeks out of the month, a
teeming resurrection in
oils thick as a sapling,
rough as a sycamore bole,
orange, blue, red, seventeen
shades of green, the crucified
woman burgeons to power.
Lucky if she doesn't
die of cancer at fifty-two, a
virgin, a lover of women they just once let touch one,
and her Muse,
bearded and placid, gets his wife pregnant again.

The Last Time

Somebody has endlessly postponed
this summer; it is chilly and uncertain
as you, my own, not in the least my own.
I watched clouds move through the organza curtain
all afternoon. The noises of the farm
and loud birds ravaging Tom's kitchen garden
break on my book. Untrustworthy, the light
shifts every hour, wind sun fog sun wind storm.
I can't blame you, or ask your pardon,
or dream the day into another night

and wake up foundering between self-pity
and despair, the way I did today,
and take a morning train back to the city
where nothing much will happen anyway,
dubious individuals will write
dubious poetry, children will get cuffed
for nothing, and not forget it, I will fault
everyone fastidiously, tight-
assed and sceptical, obscure enough
to get away with it. O could I halt

this headfirst fall and rest love in your green
approval, tasting you like certainty,
summer would certainly start, something clean
and mobile as hill winds would move with me
and I would do . . . No, I do not believe
any of this, invoke it when I fear
the dull immobile speechless bland inert
mad lady who sits in me when I leave,
comfy as anything. Through her queer
nerveless hide, nothing pleasures, nothing hurts,

she could sit in the same place all day, all day,
not seeing, not hearing, not deaf, not blind,
her eyes like marbles and her flanks like whey;
the Sow reposes sated on my mind,
sated on what would have been a clean
if bitter lyric, setting me apart
from people who can say, "I did," "I thought,"
as real things. I have said what I mean,
more than I meant; and if I start
over, from the beginning, if she bought

my silence with that other fear: you will
always be alone, I will console
you, I would have to be still
or tell lies, if I believed in a soul,
damn it, if I believed in my art, fake
it. And I will believe in that,
if necessary, as an act of will,
and she, stuporous lunatic, makes me make
poems; more than love or fame, her flat
face presses inside my face; she spills

through me, hypoglycaemic languor
paralyzing rage, her rage, my rage.
Poles: pain and insensibility, anger
and absence, the senile queen, the murdering page.
He keeps me up all night. She makes me sleep
all day. Now clogged and vague, I maul the pain
to shape. They'll never let me out. Or I'm
not going. Anyway, not off the deep
end. Lovely people, I won't come again.
This is the last time. (That was the last time.)

Prism and Lens

Prism and Lens

I

Sour hemlock dregs and bitter love
have stained the sleepless rhythms of
the pale autumnal queen who pressed
bruised leaves of broom between her breasts.
The boys of spring, their heads turned south,
with yellow flowers in their mouths;
their laurel arms and butter knees
are sucked down pristine vortices
of life that lies and death that soars
and love that breaks the lips of scars
and with inquiring fingers grinds
fresh salt into forgotten wounds
as time's equivocation locks
its knuckles on the equinox.

These nights old madwomen chant in the streets
wailing their deaths to the October dusk.
Precocious cold sullies our gelid sheets.
Our hands turn yellow, and a sticky crust
devils our eyelids wakening. The husk
of absent harvest, pallid, skyborne, beats
a shadow sheaf into the window dust.
The rats wax bold without enough to eat.

I have no cognizance of what you feel.
What do you know of me? I am alone.
The turning sockets on the rack of bone
rotate like the cogged hubs of jointed wheels.
Synaptic sparks strike from them as they run.

Beneath the water's glazed excrescences
the slow unfolding of anemones
implodes a phosphorescence on the sun
as sound breaks on the silence of the sea.
A slight deflection of the middle ear
cracks the reflected sky. I cannot hear.
Sound shatters on the long hush of the sea
as we wake on the crumbling sand, the black
landscape of dreams outlined behind our backs.

God, but I hoped the night would never end.
Still, the moon faded, and encroaching light
fingered the purple darkness into corners.
You hoisted up your coat over your shoulders,
prodding the crumbs of morning from your eyes,
closed the kitchen door softly behind you,
sleep still webbing your eyelids to their rims,
loped past a stray dog cowering on the stairs,
crossed the cold hall, opened the broken door.
It was still very early in the morning.
A calendar torn in the alleyway
washed the pavingblocks with scattered days.

Turn a familiar corner, autumn rust
limns the pavingstones with burnished scales.
A sudden shift of focus: waiting just
around the corner, just where focus fails
to mesh, the shifting point at which you must
abandon sight, a shaft of light impales
a widened shadow with a single thrust
blinding the eyes that you have ceased to trust.

II

She howls home late on strange October nights
in a hunter's jacket over a soiled pullover
with pockets full of desultory objects.
The pocked lascivious moon brings down her blood.

My mother got me awfully overdressed.
This fellow took me over in a cab.
He had red skin. His big hand, like a crab,
fumbled through my collar at my breast
and then completely disarranged my hair.
I felt three hairpins fall inside my coat
and tangle in the muffler at my throat.
I don't recall exactly who was there . . .
a boy with an emaciated face
who drank can after can of lukewarm beer
and turned away if anyone came near
or walked away to a vacated place
or took more beer from the refrigerator
and gulped it loudly on the windowsill.
"You shouldn't drink it if it makes you ill,"
I said, and he would not speak to me later.
A dark-haired girl who had the slightest lisp
who came wearing a man's blue flannel shirt
and sneakers that were decadent with dirt.
Her eyes were mellow, though her voice was crisp.
She sat off in the kitchen with a book.
I came and sat beside her, just by chance,
because I felt too out of place to dance.
Her eyes were lucent amber, when I looked.
She struck a match, and over the round flame
looked at me with a sort of open smile
that said I ought to stay and talk a while.

I happened to have overheard her name
and knew that she had been in school with X
who was, in turn, a friend of Y and Z
who were at least on speaking terms with me
so I announced myself. She looked perplexed,
then didn't look perplexed and didn't care
and talked of something trivial instead.
I saw a couple on the sofa-bed
writhing, and attempted not to stare.
I guess she saw me looking at the floor,
was quiet for a moment. Then she said
something that made me turn and lift my head.
I don't remember what though anymore.
I don't know what I said. I wish I could
remember that. Once, I stretched out my hand
and stared at it and hoped she'd understand
and tell me what I never understood
but that was what she never understood,
although I tried to say, and wasn't able.
I let my hand fall on the kitchen table
and spread my yellow fingers on the wood.

III

In the chill outer rooms of strangers' houses,
women's rearrangements or men's disorder,
with nothing that remains to do but wait,
chafing rough cold palms between the knees,
sometimes watching a corner of the ceiling,
sometimes watching a small obtrusive spider
skeletize a silken polyhedron
from a remoter corner of the ceiling.
Someone is waiting in the other room.

We sit in a cold room. A. pours the tea.
A gaudy twilight helps us hide ourselves.
I try to read the titles on the shelves
and juggle cup and saucer on my knee.
A. tells me anecdotes that I have read.
I poise a studied ambiguity.
A. wonders will I turn my head and see
the crumpled blue kimono on the bed.
I pick a crystal ashtray up to watch
its slow rotation slap a waterfall
of iridescent limbs across a wall,
fumble with cigarettes. A. strikes a match
as the enormity of darkness swells
upward in a cacophony of bells.

    IV
I will not lie and say I spent the night
calmly, ate a light meal, washed my hair,
read novels with hot coffee by my chair,
then brushed my teeth, undressed, switched off the
   light.
I came back twice to see if you were there,
and, when you weren't, left, hoping I might
walk off your absence, or walk off the tight
fist closing on my gut and cease to care;
but first I left a note that said I'd gone
walking, and I turned the lights all on.
The glancing lamps reflected my wet face
uncomprehending in a tight grimace.
I walked across the city in the rain,
river to river, then walked back again.

The sun drops quickly. Night rips the green sky.
Pale flares of incandescent mercury
drop limpid pools along the broad expanse
where shadows scatter in a jagged dance
on broken pavingstones and frozen tar,
and scarlet flashes break the flight of cars.
Dull gold in dim rooms, figures pause and pass
naked between a prism and a glass.
The lamps along the river, one by one,
spear the dark wings that hover on the sun.

Darkness and moisture settle on my cheeks.
The rain dissolves to close mist in the air.
(You sat back rigid in the easy chair,
your fingers gripped the arms. You would not speak.)
The fog thins out in front of me, revealing
careening grillwork on a tenement.
(You told me then. I wondered what you meant.
A flake of plaster crashed down from the ceiling.)
The shape of movement comes before the act,
contorts the face into a score of faces,
converts each possibility to fact.
A host of orgiastic angels come
trod me with spurious equilibrium.

V

Someone is waiting in the other room.
Someone is waiting just across the street.
Someone is waiting just beyond your sight.
The conversation comes to an impasse.
Something that ran in breathless from the cold
turns dry and measured as the hours grow old.

Word meshes word. The walls have turned to glass.
As the long instant of a touch ignites,
blurred shapes, whirled into focus by his fears,
plunge headlong down the chasm of the years.
The passing night remembers other nights.
Precluding sleep, a blanket of unease
falls on spent thighs and interlocking knees.
You shift your shoulder and avert your face
from the circumference of the embrace.
He thrusts his hands under the pillow, tries
to break the mirrors hung behind his eyes.

Here is the hub of ambiguity.
Electric spectra splash across the street.
Equivocation knots the shadowed features
of boys who are not boys; a quirk of darkness
shrivels a full mouth to senility
or pares it to a razor-edge, pours acid
across an amber cheek, fingers
a crotch, or smashes in the pelvic arch
and wells a dark clot oozing on a chest,
dispelled with motion, or a flare of light
that swells the lips and dribbles them with blood.
They say the hustlers paint their lips with blood.
They say the same crowd surges up the street
and down again, like driftwood borne
tidewise ashore and sucked away with backwash,
only to slap into the sand again,
only to be jerked out and spun away.
Driftwood: the narrow hips, the liquid eyes,
wide or thin shoulders, smooth or roughened hands,
the grey-faced jackals kneeling to their prey.
The colors disappear at break of day

when stragglers toward the west riverdocks meet
young sailors ambling shipward on the street.

You learn to know a city by its rivers,
crackling cellophane under the sun
or heaving rubber on a cloudy night,
what kind of boats haul cargo down to sea
or tug the moorings or patrol the banks,
what bridges leap across in transverse flight,
what kind of boys go prowling on the docks
or fish on Sundays with their paunchy fathers
or flash naked in summer from the pilings.

Two cops in a patrolcar came
and stopped me by the riverside.
They asked me my address, my name,
and had I thought of suicide.

"I came to watch the morning rise."
They stared in a peculiar way,
and one, appearing very wise,
said there would be no sun that day,

and girls should not stay out all night
and roam at random in the park
where deeds too warped for human sight
were perpetrated in the dark,

and midnight cold and morning chill
are detrimental to the liver,
and I had not convinced them still
I would not jump into the river,

and did not seem to be of age
for wandering at break of day
and would incur parental rage,
or else might be a runaway,

or else had fled a husband's house
to finish a nocturnal fight,
confounding the bewildered spouse
in stationhouses all the night.

"I may go drifting anyplace,
lawful and with impunity."
The headlights' glare upon my face
suggested my majority.

And when the streetlamps flickered, I
leaned on the rail and spoke no more
and watched the morning open high
bright wings across the Brooklyn shore.

A boy stood on the broad rim of concrete
that rims the churning river (this was down
a mile nearer the sea-tip of the town)
walled in on either side by empty piers.
Waves on concrete crashed thunder in our ears.
I watched him from the rain-slicked cobbled street
where sun-shot oil glistened like melted butter
and jutting shapes were coated with maroon
thicknesses of early afternoon.
A gull above the pilings circled three
perfect arcs, then headed down to sea.
The wind expostulated in the gutter.
I saw him stretch his open hand out, twist
it in again, clenched in an awkward fist.

Without shifting his feet, he turned his head,
acknowledged that he knew what I had seen.
I said to him, "Who are you?"
                          and he said,
"You know my name."
                          "That isn't what I mean."
My voice was booming underneath the rush
of water and the roaring in the sky.
His voice was still and clear within the hush
of echo.
          "I can tell you who, not why."
Not why my back impinges on your eyes,
my reaching hands impinge upon your hands.
My face wheels to the water and denies
your lengthened shadow falling where I stand.
Over the river wash, a seagull cries
against the wind, and hovers nearer land.

Three Seasons: 1944

for Baird Robinson

Squeezing his eyelids shut, he hears the squeak
of splintered pineboards in the cabin floor
as musky tropic winds finger the door.
Above his head, the white inverted peaks
of netting tacked around the metal cot
glimmer like sticky chrysalids. He thinks
he hears his parents laughing and the clink
of veined green glasses at the bar. A spot
back of his neck is itchy, and he shifts.
You see the Main House just across the lawn?
You're big now—almost five. We won't be long.
He scratches, and the slow white netting drifts
down—to smother him. He blinks, and yells,
thrusting his hands in front of him. Nails ratch
against the web that billows round to catch
his nose and mouth in gauze before he falls.
Eyelids and lips scratched to soft white that clings
like something foul, he sickeningly swings,
tangled out of the bed, above the floor
as singing cloys the air beyond the door.

Clanking a copper chatelaine of keys,
the school director told what he would teach.
Late summer woodlight splotched across their knees.
His mother's cheeks were mottled like a peach.
The shingled porch was flocked with silver beech
that made him think of pond-ice, cloudy cold.
The lintels were two arms beyond his reach.
The other boys looked serious and old.

They'd been flown out of England, she had told
him in the car, most, orphaned by the war.
He bit his nails and she began to scold.
"I'm glad that I won't see you anymore,"
he said, banging his elbow on the door
and waiting; but she didn't say a word
and then went on with what she'd said before.
But he had whispered, so she hadn't heard.

The warble of an unfamiliar bird—
he looked across the driveway with surprise.
"Young man, I don't believe you heard
a word we've said!" He rubbed his moistened eyes.
Against the sky, the spiring tops of trees
circled him into darkening filigrees.
The afternoon was busy. First he tore
his cuff on planter's wire behind a vine.
He hoped the house had attics to explore,
but those were dorms. He told a boy on line
about St. Croix, and when he would be nine.
The first-form proctor barked a reprimand.
His mother's day-dimmed taillights passed the sign
fronting the lawn before he waved his hand.

At first he missed his mother and his bike.
He had already gotten to connect
her absence with two aunts he didn't like
and Grandmother's disdain. He didn't expect
this other lack, muscular and direct.
(It was six months since he had learned to ride,
pushing off, wobbly, from a wooden block
eight times; then sudden balance, speed, and pride.
As if he had forgotten how to fly,

he fantasized, dawdling behind a book,
doing tight figure eights he hadn't tried
across his father's lawn at Sandy Hook
where he had never been since he was five.)

All the forty English boys had been
down in a low-beamed cellar, damp and black,
pressed, arms and belly against clammy back,
while sirens ripped the oilcloth shades. Between
the whine of bombers and the strafing guns,
each had decided that if anyone
should scream, or piss himself, or start to cry,
or chuck his food, there was no reason why
this should be remembered later on
upstairs, after the Jerry planes were gone.

The second time, two outbuildings were hit
and something made big potholes in the lawn.
The Board decided to evacuate.
A day before the third raid, they were gone.
The insular porched building in Vermont
held them no more than the flashed memory
of those five days; and by common consent
they didn't mention that. The foreign trees
saw troop-drills, though, and on the dorm walls scraps
of colored page approximated maps.
Exile was a schedule that they kept
whose order helped them regulate their fears
to days. Sometimes sweats broke while they slept,
but there were no blue tantrums, and no tears.

They found him young, and backward for his years,
too small, and still too scrawny for his size,
indifferent to their rituals upstairs.

At first they looked at him to clarify
the long grey hills that stared down their grey eyes,
but he was not impassable, nor stern,
and left them ample freedom to surmise
if he were stupid, mad, or taciturn,
so quick to understand, so slow to learn,
with lips and pointed chin of a tame fox
watching a rumpled winter sparrow turn
in flight from frosted tree to glaze-blurred rocks.
Once, someone found him hiding past the rocks,
pencil in blue-nailed fist, chewing his lips,
drawing on a salvaged cardboard box
the last of three tall-masted, web-rigged ships.
Most of the time he fumbled, though. He stuttered
and blushed in class when called on to recite.
He dropped tossed balls as if his palms were buttered
and never got code-words or answers right.
They watched him ominously when, at night,
clasped palms between his knees, knees drawn to chin,
he waited, lumped with blankets, for shut lights
to draw down darkness between him and them.
Perhaps if they had ever caught him in
some somber evocation in the sheets
like theirs, they would have jeered, then taken him,
proving Sin seaworthy. But he was chaste
for them, and more than chaste, lay still,
and more than still, lay rigid, as with fear
of what he might do if he moved, although
no one had shelled *his* cellar that past year.

There was a gable in the roof, from where
the exiled boys, with brass binoculars,
kept watch, by turns, for bombers in the air
and never watched the gravelled drive. Some cars

would rattle up: the postman in a jeep
with sparse mail for the teachers; headlight beams
at night—the doctor's Ford. Someone can't sleep.
Recurrent fever, or recurrent dreams.
One night he had a clear, disturbing dream:
a class held on the porch. His desk and chair
were third in the fourth row. It didn't seem
surprising that his books and pen were there
when he sat down. The rest, all standing, stared.
He woke wanting to cry, and hide, and cry.
The picture snarled into a knot and snared
under his ribs. He didn't remember why.
He hid in doodling. Four days spiralled by.
The weather was unusual for March.
Carpenters came. Since it was warm and dry,
they moved the first form math class to the porch.
The line of boys in shorts filed on the porch.
Smallest, he stood in front, studied his feet.
White light blazed broken shutters like a torch.
He went to the fourth row and took his seat.
His books were in the desk. He heard the neat
voice calling roll and places, then his name.
"Who told you where to sit?" The prickly heat
flushing his neck was almost fear, then shame.
Clasping his chilly fingers on his knees,
he watched the pink circle of faces freeze
into the iris of closing trees.

The Callers

Pads in a quilted bathrobe to the door.
Today, she is a psychiatric nurse
tending the woman on the second floor
(chronic obesity) who has perverse
fantasies that lurk in corners, squat
beneath rouged lamps. Beyond the door are three
tall cutouts in the blinking sunlight that
stand forward as she clicks the peephole. She
pads in thermal quilting to the door,
counting the slap of mules from stair to stair,
as migraine repetitions lace her, bore
needleholes where her name escapes. Thick hair
like hers falls on the dark brow of one
boy whose hands hesitate towards her. A son
of hers, remembered with a cue
for swellings and excuses. Every year
brought the bloating and another new
wrinkled disappearance.
                             "Why are you here?
Your counsellor should come this afternoon."
"I haven't had a counsellor for years,
Mother."
             "Of course you have. He'll be here soon,"
and turns, and lets them follow her upstairs.

Squat in the reddened corners of the room,
shadows fidget in adrenal haze.
She keeps it twilight while the afternoon
light bars the windowframes against the shades.
Hulking from the sofa, Walter stands

toward the ceiling, darkening the wall,
quakes and sits when they offer their hands
to him.

      "Walter, this is my son, Paul."
"I'm not Paul, Mother. I'm Thomas."
                              "Oh,
Thomas, your brother Paul is sick.
Sunday he was arrested. Do you know
Walter, my fiancé? It's so thick
in here, but I know I'll catch cold
if I open the windows," feels the chill
and tugs her sleeves down, wondering how old
he is now.

      "Raymond, Emmanuelle,
my mother."
          The man and woman near the door
come forward, smiling and severe.
New foster-parents? What have they come for?
She wonders if they want to leave him here.
They shake her hand, sit in opposing chairs
in corners like good children washed for tea.
She licks her flaking lips and pats her hair.
"Thomas, why don't you ever write to me?
I'm working as a psychiatric nurse
you know, two afternoons a month.
I had a breakdown, you know. That's the curse
our family must live with. Everyone
has problems, that's what I always say.
Like my brother's drinking. Walter here
was my patient. He feels bad today.
We're getting married when he's well, next year.
No sense in rushing, is there, that's what I
always say, no sense."

The room is bright
enough to hurt her eyes.
                    "Mother, why
was Paul arrested?"
                    "Last Saturday night
he stole ten dollars from a grocery store.
He works there afternoons, you know. He did it
for attention. I can't control him anymore.
He spent it all on candy. He admitted
he took it, to Miss Watson at the Home
he lives at. Sit there. Haven't I lost weight?"
They mustn't all look at her. Valium
calms them. Two fingers tap eight
palm-doses.
                    Thomas squats on carpeting
in the fringed pool of a lamp, Emmanuelle
above him on a straight chair, fingering
the frayed cuffs of her suede jacket. Well
out of the light, blue-eyed Raymond cracks
his knuckles softly, softly, staring
at the line of Thomas' half-turned back.
Beside her, Walter's thick fingers are tearing,
crushing, rolling cellophane. She takes
the pack of cigarettes away. Today
she drops his dosage. Apprehension makes
a sweet taste in her mouth.
                    "Now will you stay
in town a while? How long have you been here?"
Darkness climbs the ladders on the wall,
menacing the ceiling. They appear
restive this evening. She must sweep out all
the corners. Thomas is a wicked boy
to run away from home. His mother takes

the kitchen knife and four pink pills today
for nerves. What is he saying? Her headache
is coming back. Inside the china cage
cracking behind her forehead, something blots
on the carpet. He was forward for his age.
Drips on porcelain forget-me-nots.
Compose the hands. "You know your grandmother
is dead. She went mad before she died.
She always asked for you. Always. Your brother
was away. You can't escape it, that's what I
always say. Last week your uncle called
but I hung up. That man is not allowed
in my house. My doctor says that alcohol
promotes mental decay. He said that now
I can treat myself, that's what he said,
write my own prescriptions."

                     Walter prods
the sofa-cushions with his fists and spreads
his knees.

       "Good health is a gift of God,"
and God will punish sinners. Thomas was
evil like her mother. They would talk
about her in the other room, play cards
and laugh.

       "I've got to go now." Walter works
his way up to an undetermined height
and tracks his shadow to the door.

                     "Good-bye.
You'll come to dinner here on Sunday night."
He goes.

       "He's very sick, you know. He's my
patient."

       Thomas, near the woman's knee,

widens his dark eyes through vermilion shade.
"He's always been extremely kind to me.
Now we can talk, Thomas. You must stay
when Paul's counsellor visits. Will you write
to Paul? I'm too nervous now, you know.
When Betty-Mae gives me my pills at night
she writes letters for me sometimes. Do you
remember Betty-Mae?" He nods his head
out of the puddled lamplight. Ashy dusk
fingers his smooth cheeks like, as if. Instead
of chicken, Betty-Mae could do a roast
on Sunday. Suddenly she feels
bloated, floating on her back in thick
sweet syrup. No cheating between meals,
the doctor said. Downstairs, somebody knocks.

Counting the careful steps down to the door,
she plucks the robe out over her belly. They
must not be left alone too long. One more
—what—she lost count of. But today
she is a psychiatric nurse. Her hands
realign the medication tray
to allow the doorknob. A brown man
with a brown briefcase and a grey
suit:
    "I'm from the Youth Board, ma'am.

                          Your son
is on my case file."
               Once again the blaze
of unfamiliar sky charring the dun
figure before it.
          "Well, come in."
                She stays

fixed on the threshold, swaying with the street,
until he is above her on the stairs.
She turns, eyes full of ashes, with the sweet
taste in her mouth. Walking behind, she bears
herself as though her abdomen were big.
A nurse can't do that though, because it looks
bad for the patients. She wonders if her legs
have swelled. Ahead, the Youth Board worker walks
into her parlor, passing Thomas where
he watches from the doorway.
                   "Hello, sir."
"Thomas, isn't it? What are you doing here?"
"This is my mother," standing next to her.
"Well, now you're out of our hands." Near the door,
Thomas hunkers on his heels again
between the strangers, as the counsellor
walks to the couch. Pleasant to have nice men
for tea. "May I fix you some tea?"
"Thanks, I have other visits. I can't stay."
He opens up the briefcase on his knees.
"Our work comes first, that's what I always say."
He looks at her, and smiles as she sits down
beside him.
        "Your son is at La Honda Ranch
for Boys, about a half-hour's drive from town
If he does well there, he has a good chance
of coming home soon. I have photographs
to show you, of the building and the grounds.
They live better than we do, there."
                        He laughs.
"One day you must come out and look around."
In a mottled cardboard frame like lace
are five pink stucco houses in a row,

each of whose door and windows make a face
like in a picture-book her long-ago-gone
father gave her.
                    "Your boy will be in Section A
for six weeks, kept to grounds. In Section B
he can come to the city for the day
twice a month, on Sundays."
                                        "Can I keep
the picture?"
                    "If he does well in Sec-
tion A, he goes to Section B
after six weeks. Otherwise he is kept
in Section A. You can come to see
him, and the grounds, on any Sunday."
                                                "I
can't leave the house. I haven't been well. Now
I'm going back to work. I am a psychiatric
nurse, you know. How
is he doing? He's mentally ill,
you know."
                    "No, no one told me. . . ." Pad and pen
appear. "Mrs.-uh-you'll have to tell
me about this."
                    "He's been sick since he was ten.
His records are with the Youth Guidance Board."
"I'm with the Board, ma'am, and I haven't seen
evidence. . . ."
                    "My advice won't be ignored
as a professional."
                    "I haven't been
free to see your son. You may be right."
(At a gesture from Emmanuelle,
Raymond takes out cigarettes and lights

one for himself, for her, for Thomas.)
                                   "Will
you be able to provide a car
for the boy to come and visit you
on his free Sundays? In six weeks we are
transferring him to Section B where two
home visits monthly are permitted."
                                   "No,
I can't afford that. I don't drive.
My brother drives, but he is not allowed
in my house. When my mother was alive
she drove."
          "I see. Well, perhaps you can call
another parent. I suppose you'd like to know
when Thomas will be coming home."
                                   "Paul,"
softly says Thomas from the carpet.
                                   "Oh,
yes. Paul."
          "He isn't coming here.
He never lived here. He was at a Home.
He was happy there. They know him there.
He should see a priest. He is a Ro-
man Catholic."
               "I see." The ball-point dips
as she picks up the eggshell cardboard stand,
traces pink houses under her fingertips
and presses it collapsed between her hands,
flat as a filing-card. Paul is away,
and he will get a paper cup and pills
tonight at bedtime. Downstairs, Betty-Mae
is fixing supper. God the Father kills
the sinners' children. Thomas must not stay

past dark. Is it already dark?
The painted children rise outside.
                                        "Good day.
Call me if you have questions."
                                        Is the mark
already on his forehead? Thomas rises
with the stranger.
                        "You should cut your hair,
Thomas."
            He blocks the lamp, revivifies
arachnid dark congealing under chairs.
They go out on the landing. Who will dance
in lapping spotlights on the street tonight?
Raymond looks toward the doorway, rubbing his hands.
Emmanuelle, smoking in the lamplight,
lifts her head and smiles. They both smile,
and Thomas insubstantially returns
like something that will move a little while
and then be still. This hunger, how it burns
under her heart. It's almost suppertime.
The three are standing, Thomas facing her,
a glowing shape on either side of him,
cutting scorched paths back to where they were
sitting. They can't come for her here. She lives
here. Everything went so well today.
She was a Nurse. She'll tell them she forgives
Thomas. . . .
            "Mother, we have to leave."
                                        They go away.

Alone, she tours around the room three times,
checking the placement of the figurines
and china cups. Behind the crystal chimes,

she finds the seven caps of Thorazine
she hid from Betty-Mae. Out of her sleeve,
she takes the picture of the Ranch for Boys
and sets it on the mantel. Streetlights weave
the wall. She draws the drapes to dull the noise.

The Companion

Everywhere you are coaxing the mad
boy into your room. You offer him
cold meat and beer. You light the fire
or the stove or the electric grate.
It is always cold. The winter city
solidifies under pale sun. The street
is full of little knots of gossiping
men. He crouches on your narrow bed,
cracking his knuckles in his lap. His hair
is dirty, falling in his eyes. His eyes
are muddy, fixed on you. You sit
cross-legged on the floor next to the grate,
chain-smoking, eating a yellow pear
down to the core. It is all gone. What will
you say to him? He has nothing to say
to you, staring at his large red hands. He is
not real. His baggy olive corduroys
are frayed through at the knees. You watch his knees
for some fraternal gesture. Now your face
is sweating. Every pore glistens with oil.
His cheeks are pocked. He knows about your dream.
There is nothing he can tell you, but you watch
his arms, his tense neck, scrawl an alphabet
older than birds' teeth on the patchy wall.
He is evidently used to ladies
alone in patchy rooms, used to ladies
who come home from work and staple tapestries
no one will ever see on the blue ceiling
above the bed, used to ladies
with plants, cats, paintings, Gordon's Gin and pills.

He has no double. Objects come in pairs:
shoes, lamps, gloves, couples dining at tables
for two, policemen, telephone repairmen, nuns,
sailors on leave. But you and he are no
pair. Peach-stone of solitude, he is
cracking his knuckles in your head, suggesting
only what you told him, drinking your beer,
eating your words, eating your sweaty hours,
bargaining eyes for time, trading his pain
for your sleep, all without a word
you can remember. You will look for words
in his ears, under his chewed nails, between his livid,
thin shanks. You will look for words
accrued behind the posters on the wall,
clogging the sink-drain, in the frying-pan
sticky with last night's curry, in a glass,
an ashtray, a green sock under the bed.
Objects crawl with words, rupture their pairs,
pile up between you. He gets easily
drunk. You too. You are my family
after all, pouring on the gin,
little brother, enigmatic cousin,
mother's sky-blue boy. Must every lover
leave you here, demanding plastic screen
of what an everyday good lady wants?
No lover though, no novel, no landscape
intimating frenzy. Curtains and walls.
He leaves. Next morning you are on a train
nearing the sea. Rose dawn beyond Marseilles
and 5 AM awakenings are normal
on trains. Perhaps it was his dream
you forgot this morning; vision of
your mind, a cheesecloth or a teastrainer

that nightmares filter through. Midnight gut pain,
cold tiles, boots, darkness, to the john next door,
then lying in the morning garden, under
a cherry tree, faint whining of a loom
inside the house, a leather-cheeked old man
with a blue beret, hunching for violets
in the next field. I tricked you, Little Brother,
enclosed you in my belly. I will not
produce you here. Little Brother
waits after dinner in the outlanders'
cafe, drinking a marc and Schweppes,
looking like that Austrian émigré
with the peculiar eyes. You leave your friends
stroking each other's knees and gossiping,
to sit with him. He still has nothing
to say. The thick white saucers
pile up. You lean against the heater.
Last Saturday, one hundred forty-seven
adolescents burned to death, clawing the nailed-
shut fire exit of a thé-dansant:
Grenoble. The kids shout in the room next door,
drinking beer and roasting chestnuts, dancing
badly. They have the elegant thin bones
of Leonardo angels, last year's slang.
Most of them are fourteen. Little Brother
is hitchhiking to Carcassonne. One boy,
pale as a mushroom thinking a blonde moustache,
rests his clubbed right foot in a workhorse boot,
reversed, against the bar rail, watching.
What makes you think a cripple ought to know
any better. Sentimental bitch.
And goes, and you rejoin your friends. You wish
your train would come. Tomorrow your train comes.

You wish some enterprising sorcerer
would save a niche in his pentangular
observatory for you. Angular
and shy in the muse's naked outfit, he
enfolds you in the corporeal star
where Little Brother, scarlet in your head
and smug, still can't prank swords into your bed.
The train curves up abruptly from the sea
and you veer up from your unlikely wish
into a windowful of scenery.
I'll bring the loaves, my old. You'll fry the fish.
It's L.B. come to keep you company.
Was that your pincushion under the seat
last night? Silent before, now garrulous;
you wish he'd shut his face and put his feet
down. Mais quelle gueule! Built like a bus
you are, and with a face like runny cheese
this morning. Pitiful. Cat got your sleep?
The Dijonnais truck-salesman plants his knees
on either side of yours, leans forward. Keep
two conversations going, c'est pas chouette.
You could do without both, and watch the rilled
blade of the Rhone cut valleys. Etiquette:
answer, smile, don't throw things. Have you killed
your mother yet? Boys weaned on paradox
bore me. Go away. He goes away,
leaving the commerçant in purple socks
leering. He's kept that leer on since Marseilles.
He left you alone in Venice. Silent,
as the grey water slurped the dirty white
carved landings, you rode the vaporetto like
other tourists, watching the hollow stage-
set city retreat to Tintoretto's age,

or Byron's, more nostalgic, less remote.
Scummed winter water nibbled on the boat
shoring at the Ferrovia where you
present yourself again at almost dawn
for drizzling Florence in the afternoon.
Now, in another room, you see yourself
putting a bowl of milk beside the door,
hanging up garlic from the moulding, learning
Greek. You could be crouching by the fire
with an unopened book, again redoing
your last spoiled scene, washing your hair again,
washing the dishes, washing your face, bemused in
your own bad smell. Instead you set
a pint of bitter and some sandwiches
out on the coffee-table with your borrowed
typewriter. Everywhere you are
coaxing him into your room.

Separations

Separations

I

Satisfied lovers eat big breakfasts. I
want black coffee and a cigarette
to dull this cottonmouth. Nine-ten. The wet-
faced construction workers hunkered by
the Pioneer Grill grin as I walk past.
You tried to be sleeping when I left
your room. The sweaty blanket hugged the cleft
between your buttocks. Now a crowd of fast
clouds scutters across the cautious sky
above the Fillmore West. We didn't make
it this time. Maybe it will take
another year. If you still want to try.
We try, and fail again, and try, and fail.
I'll be back home an hour before the mail.

II

Girl we describe most littoral to life
of sliding surfaces, the nectarines
and Nordic peach live more within their means
in yellow wicker than you do. Not wife,
lover or mother, incidental friend,
scrabbler for fame, income uncertain, form
too strong in verse, too weak in body. Warm
oversoon and oversprung to bend.
Instruct me in the compass of my knees,
say I, and when was I last rude
to whom, who since has firmly shut the door?
I mean, love me and I will listen for
your voice, do not and your carpings intrude
on my direction. Pointed as I please.

III

I'm putting words into your mouth again
instead of toes or fingers, breast or tongue.
I lust after my lust when I was young,
specific tastes of unspecific men
on definitely seasoned afternoons,
and chewing on the certainty of fame
arriving at multisyllabic-named
places, suave and polyglot and soon.
And the nostalgia of the underripe
for episodes when they were even greener,
and perpetrated ambiguities
on hairy kids for amorality's
sake. Now the confusion is deeper, leaner,
but after-imaged with the same-hued stripe.

IV

And underneath a phthisic honesty
shivers I gave you all this, I, I,
the undernourished fishy female cry
on learning muses don't get royalties.
Words like the dripping faucet in the sink
erode familiar runnels in my brain:
I like being alone and I like pain.
I'm safe clutching old feelings when I think.
The open oven hisses at my back.
I linger in the kitchen, warm as soup,
and will not walk across town to the bar
where homosexual barbed poets are
repeating confrontations in a loop
circuit gossip will edit and play back.

V

This is a high and sprawling wooden flat
with seven rooms, three tenants, and four beds.
We all nurture each other in our heads
and keep our distances outside of that.
Each cares for his own plants and his own cat;
we all like gossip, magic, plots and food
and spending half a day on last night's mood
or conversation or delicious brat.
We all are vague with anger and affection.
I love them both, and not for power or sex,
and if they love me I am fortunate,
and if they love each other they'll debate
themselves; but we have saved each other's necks
for risking in more challenging directions.

VI

I still balk at my preference for rhyme
which hounds me like an inarticulate
and homely lover whom I wish would wait
outside; no, he can meet my friends this time,
screw vanity, I love him, he's my own
obsession. Voice: you clever girls and boys
may hear a kid stomping and making noise
because she's scared left in the house alone.
I set the midnight table for a new
unfledged muse, my dream-wounded animus
whose boots scuff up the stairs now. Angular
child, I have to tell them who you are,
and love you so much they will envy us
and want you so much they will want you too.

VII

I'll dabble in specifics in my bath,
fingering soap and dirt off pinkened skin.
"Someday when I'm notorious and thin,
supple in love, magnificent in wrath . . ."
Someday when I'm a lady nearing thirty,
who diets and has not had sex for weeks,
acne and crowsfeet fighting for my cheeks,
I'll wish my mind, and not my feet, were dirty.
I lean back in the tub, but now it's not
hot enough. I scrub my soles, and wish
Manhattan midnight steamed outside, and I
could go out coatless while the smoggy sky
simmered a river dawn of oil and fish
to take a walk with you. I can't. Now what?

VIII

I don't count up days of your absence; they
are of two kinds, either alike or not.
I do the same day's work in the same spot,
sun slanting on the desk across the bay
window, and stop for lunch when Brodecky
gets up; we talk, how was the bar last night,
what's in the mail, more coffee, was I right
about him, I always thought, did she?
Sometimes I go out later, or I feed
guests, and if I'm lucky, we converse.
It wouldn't be much different if you were
here, because you aren't living here.
You'd come, we'd talk, feel better, or feel worse.
You'd leave, I'd go to bed, alone, and need.

IX

Most circumspect good friend, if, by "deceive,"
you mean keep secret who is in his bed,
trust that name, age, etcetera, were said
collect over Long Distance. I believe
in Higher Gossip, shifting states of soul
revealed in nervous tics, beer and bons mots:
what do you think he thinks, I want to know,
and feels, and is maintaining in control.
And I am fairly confident that he
would also want to know that sort of thing,
at the most cynical, because he craves
reassurance I still misbehave.
O Doubtful Thomas, stop malingering
and tell me what he's saying about me!

X

You're on the telephone from far away,
and we talk money. Meaning love, or food?
You disapprove of me. I think I should
not have to lop off blackmail from my pay.
I don't like taking handouts, and I don't
like you turning something I have earned
into a handout. Maybe I have learned
I'm competent. I'll make it, or I won't.
I'm burning with displeaseds and disapproves.
Let's fight like lovers if we have to fight
and gouge these holes from rage or jealousy.
You mean to hurt, and you are hurting me,
not drafting texts on what is good and right.
I am in pain, but I am still in love.

XI

I struggle up from sleep into the fog-
gy morning, grey again today, the grey
routine of absence permeates the day.
I shove the pillows off. A dialogue
continues that was started in a dream
where you were scolding me for being cold
to someone. Bath. The poems are not cold.
Coffee. It is trivial to scream
forever. Later I must write to you.
We go to North Beach to rehearse the play.
I fix myself a sandwich and a drink,
arrange the desk for working, while I think,
"Three weeks from now this will be far away."
The doorbell rings. The night is something new.

XII

And if my compass straggles to your chest's
ferrous tangle and I dock again
seaworthy on your salt, love, lave me then
gently of seagrime. Hold me and let me rest.
Inquire where the erosions and the scars
come from, and if I am cradled well
out of the wind, I possibly will tell
the truth. While my conceit consults the stars
to navigate, I, not metaphor,
am informed by distance. You become
this journey, as eye-sockets define
vision. Distance finishes the line
and shapes a destination for the poem
while I plot courses toward a human harbor.

XIII

The letter that I want to write to you
is problematical for me to start.
I try to gauge how far we are apart
and see a vast parenthesis. The blue
sky tautens behind the morning haze.
The mountains will be visible by noon.
Downstairs, the twins make applesauce and croon
French songs they learned at camp. In four more days
I'll start out for Toronto on the train.
Two cities more, then one for both of us,
and then, as Alice said, "I'll be too far
away." It frightens me to think you are
two weeks away. We will have to pass
carefully. And separate again.

XIV

Friend (this is an imaginary letter
to someone I don't know), out of the hewn-
rock mountains, with the muddy morning rain
raising steam on spring-pools (but a scatter
of snowfields on the peaks), the train descends
to prairies looking shabby under storm
blankets. I am eating bread and cheese
to stretch two dollars out over three days.
(Vancouver was extravagant.) I'm warm
jackknifed under my fur. The train's growl blends
with nightsounds of old men, babies, a plains-
woman's beery laugh. Legs cramped, I go
to sleep, rocked by a Cree kid's radio
wailing blues' soulsolace on the night train.

XV

And here we are, or rather, here am I;
hungover, headachy, insomniac.
The clock rings four. I turn onto my back.
Four-thirty. Five. Wet traffic whispers by
Thamesward. I've been in London for
twelve hours now. It's already getting light.
I sit up, take my notebook, try to write
ten reasons not to see you anymore.
One: you will hurt me; Two: you will resent
my hurt; Three: but I light a cigarette
and sit against the wall and smoke instead,
thinking of times I've been kicked out of bed
and suffered O. Tired, as the curtains get
pale, I write this, and sleep all morning, spent.

XVI

Culled from the brambled ceiling of my wide-
eyed latternights, he spends the afternoon
across the room, quiet at first, but soon
proffering novels about suicide
and madness in instructional detail.
This is the way it's done. Watch every crack
in the soiled wall flap open and coax back
your eyes to where I stand, a limber, pale
absence. Dead woman, you are not my twin;
why do we have a brother, following
me to foreign cities, saying: make
words, make noise, make time, tonight you'll wake
staring in halflight, sweating, lingering
under my cold suggestions on your skin.

XVII

Only constant in his absence, he's
month-faced as Mother, face turns into face
into an alphabet of features, piece-
meal, reconstituted mysteries
served up for supper on a heavy plate,
cracked down the center with his morning smile.
The trains clack like a drummer out of style;
the gas-red ball slides down the chimney. Wait
beside the heater, thumbing through a stack
of crumpled papers on financial schemes.
Numbers drop to the rug; strands of loose hair
drop to the rug; an eye, a thumb, an ear
pile desultorily between my knees. It seems
none of the faces will be coming back.

XVIII

A February of the merely real,
plumbers, not bayonets, outside the door,
colds, personal despair. I wrote, "The war
is far away," back to Perine Place reel-
ing and sick with tear-gas from a taut
poets-cum-journalists' soirée. The shades
were drawn. We joked about the barricades,
listening to gunfire. I got caught
by a bugmask's canister on Haight.
Sinecured exiles with unfunny eyes
converge on the Cultural Attache's
free whisky, playing Corner Points for praise.
It's hard to tell the poets from the spies.
The war is far away. Will wait. Will wait.

TAKING NOTICE

Feeling and Form

Feeling and Form

for Sandy Moore and for Susanne K. Langer

Dear San: Everybody doesn't write poetry.
A lot of people doodle profiles, write
something they think approximates poetry
because nobody taught them to read poetry.
Rhyming or trailing gerunds, clumps of words
straggle a page, unjustified—poetry?
It's not like talking, so it must be poetry.
Before they learn to write, all children draw
pictures grown-ups teach them how not to draw.
Anyone learns/unlearns the craft of poetry
too. The fourth grader who gets a neat like-
ness of Mom in crayon's not unlike

the woman who sent you her Tone Poem, who'd like
her admiration praised. That isn't poetry,
unless she did the work that makes it like
this, any, work, in outrage, love, or lik-
ing an apple's October texture. Write
about anything—I wish I could. It's like
the still-lives you love: you don't have to like
apples to like Cezanne. I do like words,
which is why I make things out of words
and listen to their hints, resounding like
skipping-stones radiating circles, draw-
ing context from text, the way I've watched you draw

a pepper shaker on a table, draw
it again, once more, until it isn't like
anything but your idea of a draw-
ing, like an idea of movement, draw-
ing its shape from sequence. You write poetry.

I was a clever child who liked to draw,
and did it well, but when I watch you draw,
you rubber-face like I do when I write:
chewed lip, cat-tongue, smiles, scowls that go with right
choices, perplexed, deliberate, withdrawn
in worked play, conscious of the spaces words
or lines make as you make them, without words

for instant exegesis. Molding words
around a shape's analogous to draw-
ing these coffee-cups in settings words
describe, but whose significance leaves words
unsaid, because it's drawn, because it's like
not my blue mug, but inked lines. Chosen words
—I couldn't write *your white mug*—collect words
they're meant, or drawn to, make mental space poetry
extends beyond the page. If you thought poetry
were merely nicely ordered private words
for two eyes only, why would you say, "Write
me a letter, dammit!" This is a letter, right?

Wrong. Form intimates fiction. I could write
me as a mathematician, weave in words
implying *you* a man, sixteen, a right-
handed abstract expressionist. I'd write
untruths, from which some other *you* could draw
odd inferences. Though I don't, I write
you, and you're the Donor on the right-
hand panel, kneeling in sable kirtle. Like-
ly I'm the lady left of you, who'd like
to peer into your missal, where the writ-
ing (legible Gothic) lauds in Latin poetry
the Lady at the center. Call her poetry,

virtual space, or Bona Dea. Poetry
dovetails contradictions. If I write
a private *you* a public discourse, words
tempered and stroked will draw you where you draw
these lines, and yours, convergent, made, unlike;

that likelihood draws words I write to poetry.

Living in the Moment

Sequence

1

A woman is talking to you. You represent
only yourself, usual, unique:
a man half listening to a woman speak
words also about words. You are absent;
you are silent. If I tried to fake
disinterested reason, I would fail.
I've smoked so much my mouth is rank and stale.
I've drunk enough to be just half awake.
If you walked in I wouldn't know what to do.
Damn them and their freedom, said my friend,
her lover off to Greece, Chip teaching child-
free seminars, you, your car piled
with books, approaching Penzance or Ostend,
and beside you, a woman is talking to you.

2

(Black Mountains, early March)

Rocks, heather, mud, veered up from either side
of the thin road like a crease between hills.
Stout ponies munched the scrub. We were chilled
through with the fine rain, even inside
your heavy car, but I gasped with a child's
joy at the breadth and height of that wild place.
The car's broad jaw crunched branch. Your clenched face
gripped the road, when it was clear, you smiled
at the road if not at me, peopled the crags
with relatives and friends, and then with loss
of which you didn't speak. Rain splats, talk sags.
I watched you and the hills, twice alien.
Needles of light ravelled the clouds. A cross-
post pointed us back to London again.

3

Beautiful to me, you have lived in it long
enough to think, I think, any song
in your body's praise puerile. You never loved yourself
much, howevermuch I love your face
when your mouth cracks free from gloom, unexpected grace
across a room, at an overfilled bookshelf.
I'd like to make you words as physical
as waking with hungry skin, an extravagant
shudder to touch, like a branchy plant
palming the window with bright leaves. Beautiful,
but who wants one, these starved days being rational
and rationed out? You are very real
when I dream you into bed; you feel
for the misplaced key, and drive off, as usual.

4

Across unmeasured distances between
proximities, you find me anyway
easily. What comes over me, the way
I come over you? Well enough left alone,
but I'm not. Once I could celebrate
the darkness we collided in; how much
more difficult to parse some sense to touch-
ing a friend in daylight. Recapitulate:
tragedians accept the Status Quo
as a Good Thing, try to alter it and go
to the waiting dogs, however nobly. We
will not be tragic heroes, love, okay?
I think the status quo has had its day.
Revolutions feed on comedy.

5

Solemn, unfunny, earnest, doctrinaire,
I grip you in a four-hour verbal wrangle
as we postpone another sort of tangle.
We smoke. I twist my legs around the chair-
legs (hoping that they will wind
later with yours), light up from butts. We drink.
Do I bother to find out what you think?
You'll say that you can't say what's on your mind
(or don't I ask till we're too drunk to care?)
Towards morning, in the wordless dark upstairs
our hands and mouths continue discourse, guide
us sometimes to a meeting. While the birds
wake up, we sleep. Naked, I lie beside
you, naked, with a head still full of words.

6

What good are words if none of them can free
us from our imagined selves? You are
one man, not some indifferent Muse to me.
(We women poets have no stock of far-fetched
icons to keep you suitably far
from our aggrandized passions.) Can we see
beyond the ineffectual crass caricatures
the mirror limns when we
have learned from lovers, analysts and B
movies we aren't what we ought to be?
Guilt, loneliness, self-pity, jealousy,
bound from the words I tweak for poetry,
and hung back, graceless, words that say we are
not free, but more free than we'd like to be.

7

But this, five days ago a baby died
should not have died, healthy, loved, cared-
for by her one mother, too prepared
for loss by loss. I am blank inside
as the child loses her name. No one will say:
Lucy Aviva Scott, in her twelfth week,
died in her crib. Too cowardly to speak,
I write, and my gut convulses while I play
with my loud live child. But this: how can I be
free, with a spoilt obscenity of choice,
reasonably whole, reasonably sane,
if I cannot look at the torn pain and the numb pain
lived in, not out; only with a hushed voice
blank out the dead child too sharp to see?

8

My bat-eared baby sleeping bottom up,
your three sons with their mother's copper hair,
hold us to our wished selves, hostage to their
futures. There the resemblance stops,
at a rift between memory and change.
I don't trust the lost past you'd like to save;
my brave alternatives you'd call a Brave
New World, raw and discomforting and strange.
I called her Lucy because when we were
in Sweden, there was a kind of midwinter
queen, called Lucy. There was a feast for her
on the shortest day, to give you hope. That's why
she was Lucy, for light on a dark day.
Choice is a gift. Choice is a luxury.

The Regent's Park Sonnets

1

"That was in another country," but the wench
is not yet dead, parks the red-striped pushchair
near the Rose Garden and turns loose her fair
Black Jewish Woman Baby; picks a bench
scoured by warm winds; (five years ago, twelve days
and nights, another country, where the might-
be was incarnated every night),
squints, focussing on the child, not yours, who plays
explorers. You are in another count-
ry, house-guesting, annual August rounds
as solid as ripe apples, on the grounds
of continuity, convenience (*Con!*
suggests itself; it seems I can't be hon-
est and not too bitter or too blunt).

2

You rang me up this morning from Marseilles
echoing other lines and other lives.
The best-intentioned women sound like wives
sometimes: why couldn't I find something to say
but "When will you be back?" Above the play-
ground, like a capsuled world, a plane
heads, fortunately, north. Fresh after rain
the sky is innocently blue. Away
from frisking kids, including mine, I write
stretched on a handkerchief of pungent dry
grass, wishing I could take off my shirt.
I word old wounds. As usual, they hurt
less. Iva's giving someone's bike a try.
We could be on a plane tomorrow night.

3

Some table-talk at lunch, of memory:
the anecdotal hypnotist who could
unlock the nursery. Not babyhood
occurred to me, but two weeks buried by
the next five years. That's when I should have made
poems each extraordinary day
and I could read them now and brush away
the dust accrued over a half-decade,
and I'd remember everything we said
when I thought we were saying everything.
We did, I guess, what everybody does,
if I were better at remembering.
Sometimes I wonder who I thought I was
and who on earth I thought was in my bed.

4

"What's in a park they warn girls out of?" "Queers."
That's what I thought of parks at seventeen:
hunting-grounds, pleasure-gardens, never seen
by day eyes, girls' eyes, blinkered eyes like theirs—
the clucking mums on benches near the swings.
I've joined their number after fifteen years.
I'm sure behind the bushes after hours
all sorts of lewd and fascinating things
still happen. But they won't happen to me.
If I were tall and tan and twenty-three,
I still would be a woman. So I stay
among women and children, on the day
side, guarding a blue pail and red spade.
I wonder how they manage to get laid?

5

One master, aged, as I am, thirty-two,
all summer sonneted adulterous
love: cocktails and woods, fortuitous
meetings, public words that no one knew
were private. This playground is an odd land-
scape for longings in an afternoon
splashed with babies' bright clothes. Near six now. Soon,
grown tired of high adventure in the sand-
pit, we will head for home and food.
We—you and I—don't have a thing to hide.
We need not meet through pseudonyms and gin.
Yet there's no common space for meeting in,
and secrets fence me in on every side.
This week is taking longer than it should.

6

Another poet, woman and alive,
recalls: sorrow is politics. Another
woman, not my tormentor, not my mother,
waits for you, in a castle. Gosh! We thrive,
it seems, on *Woman's Own*. On women's own
solitude, uncertainty, old fears
nursed, like a taste for brandy, over years.
"If you don't mind, I'd still rather not know
you." Wound like clockwork, she and I,
speechless, oppose. Central, you stroke one, strike
the other. In New York, I lived with two
men; we loved each other. Do you *like*
either? Replaceable, we know it, sigh,
resigned, while options preen in front of you.

7

Thursday, the eighth of August, four o'clock.
Fire-salvaged wood desk filled the window bay,
notebook, cat curled round coleus: the way
I spent those afternoons. Downstairs, a knock.
Midnight at the Savoy-Tivoli
still talking; me guilty you paid the bill
while I was in the john. Bar, home, alone, still
dazed. Paul and Bill: "Have you noticed he's
most attractive?" "Oh, shut up!" Ninety-one
degrees today, in London. On the dock
flushed kids queue for canoes. Iva, in bright
blue shorts, clambers the bench. On Friday night
hands brushed in the dark, stayed: finished, begun.
—Friday, the eighth of August, four o'clock.

8

Gino's hummed an epithalamion:
one resident fag-hag and paedophile
reformed! You knocked *Jack Daniel's* back in style.
In two days you would go and fetch your son.
Meanwhile bought rounds. I think groped Nemi's knee.
I almost minded. Under the table, gripped
my legs in yours. "Let's go." My cronies quipped
farewells. (The pub downstairs, less leisurely,
disgorges footsteps and unsteady songs
bracketed by cars.) Late through the long
night, our tongues grappled in a double cave.
Naked swimmers plunged in wave over wave,
hands, mouths, loins, filling and filled, until we gave
ourselves back, tired, seawashed and salty, strong.

(CODA)

It was not my mother or my daughter
who did me in. Women have been betrayed
by history, which ignores us, which we made
like anyone, with work and words, slaughter
and silver. "The Celts treated their women well . . ."
(I guess their wives were Picts.) A man at a table—
like you, whose face is etched on my nights, unable
to see as I see that first face first in hell-
ish uncertainties, and then unlearn, relearn.
The peach-faced Cypriot boy brings us more wine.
Cryptic, perhaps, yes, as this hedged return.
I choke up, as if I had breathed water.
Other, not polar, not my mother or daughter.
Some woman might have understood the line.

Part of a Letter

Poems I wrote you in Tourrettes
are in anthologies.
I've given up French cigarettes.
I stand and watch the trees

silver-boled and sprocketed
with infant April green,
fists of jonquils pocketed
in dry branch in between,

blown and jostled up the slope
soundless beyond the case-
ment's seal. My bus was late. She hoped
after I'd washed my face

—here was my room—and had a rest,
I'd join them downstairs. "We've
a cocktail party for the guest
poets in forty-five

minutes." Square beige rugs—twenty feet—
two beds, desk, mirrors, view,
five lamps, a quiet source of heat,
a bathroom tiled dark blue,

outdo Amsterdam Avenue,
certainly Marylebone.
Thousands of miles away from you,
all this past week I've gone

from bus to bus to common room
of questioning scrubbed faces:
Why do you have this running theme
of exile? In what places

do you write best? Do poets earn
a living? How? Where can
I publish? Can a woman learn
writing from a man?

Dusk, and I henscratch this to you
which, after you have seen
it, may meet more public view
in some small magazine,

which doesn't make the distance hurt
less, or me less tender—
both senses. Now, in a clean shirt,
to drinks with Mr. Spender.

Rondeau after a Transatlantic Telephone Call

Love, it was good to talk to you tonight.
You lather me like summer though. I light
up, sip smoke. Insistent through walls comes
the downstairs neighbor's double-bass. It thrums
like toothache. I will shower away the sweat,

smoke, summer, sound. Slick, soapy, dripping wet,
I scrub the sharp edge off my appetite.
I want: crisp toast, cold wine prickling my gums,
love. It was good

imagining around your voice, you, late-
awake there. (It isn't midnight yet
here.) This last glass washes down the crumbs.
I wish that I could lie down in your arms
and, turned toward sleep there (later), say, "Goodnight,
love. It was good."

Living in the Moment

"This is a seasick way,
this almost/never touching, this
drawing-off, this to-and-fro."
ADRIENNE RICH: *"The Demon Lover"*

Two blue glasses of neat
whiskey, epoxy-mended Japanese
ashtray accruing Marlboro and Gauloise
butts, umber and Prussian blue ceramic cups
of Zabar's French Roast, cooling. You acquired
a paunch; I am almost skinny
as I'd like to be. You are probably
right, leaving. We've been here
thousands of miles away, hundreds of times before.

I try to be a woman I could love.
I am probably wrong, asking
you to stay. Blue cotton jersey
turtleneck, navy corduroy Levi's,
nylon briefs, boy's undershirt, socks, hiking shoes:
inside (bagged opals, red silk swaddles a
Swiss Army knife) a body nobody sees.
Outside, cars and men screech on Amsterdam Avenue
hundreds of times, before, thousands of miles away,

hidden in cropped hair like a lampshade,
I try to say what I think I mean.
My thirty-five-year-old white skin wants you
to stroke back twenty-seven-yezar-old certainty
I'd better doubt. The time-stopped
light hours ago on the smelly East River
glazes my eyes with numbers, years. We both

wear glasses. We both have children
thousands of miles away. Hundreds of times before,

we agree, the nerves' text tricked us
to bad translation. My wrapped sex cups
strong drink. A woman honed words
for this at an oak desk above the Hudson
River in November; cross-legged on woven straw
in a white room in a stucco house; locked
in the bathroom away from the babies, notebook
on her knees. I repeat what we were asking
hundreds of times before. Thousands of miles away,

I am leaving you at Heathrow. Revolution
of a dozen engines drowns parting
words, ways: "I should be asking you to stay."
I shouldn't be asking you to stay. We finish
our courage. Tumblers click on the table.
Tumblers click in the lock. I unwrap
cotton and corduroy, nylon and cotton,
wrap up in flannel for the night that started
thousands of miles before, hundreds of times away.

Burnham Beeches

At two A.M., chain-smoking in your car,
I unironically must praise you for
choosing an overdue fidelity
to someone who has got no use for me.

We might have used each other if we could.
Lost at late twilight in an ancient wood,
we are not changed much on Midsummer's Eve.
We spiral miles to find the car and leave.

Inhabited or not, the present trees
incorporate us in mythologies;
we think they do as they bulk out in ours
—I should say "I" and "mine." Indifferent powers,

boled Bona Dea, Druid patriarch,
nor mock nor bless in the forestalled half-dark.
I flesh them with what separates us: sex,
as we sit on a log, just out of reach

of each other's reminiscent hands.
Rain slants the last light through sibilant branches.
We scuff out cigarette butts on the ground,
turn up our collars and retrieve the road.

I hope we shared the manna of the place.
I choose to praise your necessary choice
that nothing was engendered in the wood
but powers that would have changed us if they could.

Adult Entertainment

Agreed: Familiarity breeds
confusion; cautious consistency is better.
You would be harried; I (and she) be hurt.
Sane speaking distance is safest and best.

Under an academic tweed
jacket, over a second-hand Shetland sweater,
a cotton jersey and an undershirt,
your naked hand welcomes my naked breast.

A Man with Sons

for David Batterham

You come back with a heaped shopping basket:
a huge romaine, a wholemeal loaf, tomatoes.
You put a big chipped saucepan on to boil,
dip the tomatoes on a ladle. "What
are you doing to them, Dad?"
The eighteen-year-old looks up from his letter.
"Taking off their skins." Nonfunctional,
I straddle a wooden chair, watch
you sieve the scalded, peeled pulp-globes
into (you tell us) last night's fish broth.
My friend's just made her way here from the Tube,
climbs from the lower room, contentedly
ungloving book-dust from her elbows, adds
cadenza to the kitchen colloquy.
My stomach calms an octave into speech.
Stained mugs, newspapers straggle off the table
as the boys straggle in. One, fourteen
looking ten, overalled, leaves
a postcard album on a cluttered shelf.
Svelte in T-shirt as your bronze Florentine
namesake, the questioning middle one makes room
for his leather-jacketed, apricot-cheeked friend
who lives here too. The twenty-year-old
painter, slicked back damp from summer job
lifeguarding, eye-sockets blackberry blotches:
"I got in a fight. Really, I got fought on.
Who wants," he slices, back to us, "some bread?"
Now there is a salad on the table,
green, orange, purple, frilling a wooden bowl.
You plunk down odd plates, ceramic porringers

your brother made. If an ailanthus tree
strained through the splintery floorboards, it would be me,
leaf-pores dilated toward you, perhaps because
this is complete without me. Pouring water, you pose
inadvertently, with the two younger boys
bent toward your chair. The big window behind
the table frames you with a bricked-in garden
where a transplanted pet's five-fingered leaves
stretch to the light. My friend, mother of sons,
pours warm baritone laughter on the banter
like burgundy. Milk, water, Coca-Cola
gurgle in glasses. She roots me
(boy-lover once, once your lover, a daughter's
mother) to the other plot I garden
weeding out nostalgia. Your soup is good
as your boys' voices, bread shared on a board
(as little or as much as we can share).
I weigh the paradox of praising you
for what, unpraised, daily, most women do,
a praise, a paradox I can't afford.
You heap my plate with salad, wedge of bread,
after my friend's, before your youngest's; then
the grown boys amicably seize the bowl.
Made adversaries by tired ironies
at midnight, failures of nerve, failures of charity,
bad actors in humiliating roles:
primeval woman, archetypal man,
who clutch, abandon, claim, betray, demand;
friends in noon's grace we are forgiven, whole.

The Hang-Glider's Daughter

Prayer for My Daughter

You'll be
coming home alone on the AA
Local from Canal St., 1 A.M.
Two black girls, sixteen, bushy
in plaid wool jackets, fiddle
with a huge transistor radio.
A stout bespectacled white woman reads
Novy Mir
poking at a grey braid.
A thin blue blonde dozes on shopping bags.
Tobacco-colored, hatchet-faced and square,
another mumbles in her leather collar.
Three sharp Latinas jive round the center-post, bouncing
a pig-tailed baby, tiny sparkling
earrings, tiny work overalls.
A scrubbed corduroy girl wearing a slide-rule eyes
a Broadway redhead wearing green fingernails.
A huge-breasted drunk, vines
splayed on cheeks, inventively
slangs the bored brown
woman in a cop suit, strolling.
You'll get out at 81st St. (Planetarium)
and lope upstairs, travelling light-years.
The war is over!

Boulder: August 1977

Curves converge and blossom in your face;
leaf-shapes ripple a patterned snake
safe through pied grass. A tacky diamondback
linoleum, earth, russet, green, and black,
covers my rented table. Typescript heaps
await parenthesis between our sleeps.
You're asleep now, murmuring, in the other room.
The mountain range has a domestic name;
I am domesticated at its foot,
flabby, diasporid, illiterate
in lichens, grasses, insects, conifers.
Here is a white man lettering AFRICA
on a scrapbook of Tarzan movie stills.
Reading it is my work. A woman whirls
her nightgowned daughter on her hip. Night gowns
them, whirls them, us, through different windows, down.

Three Sonnets for Iva

He tips his boy baby's hands in an icy
stream from the mountaintop. The velvet cheek
of sky is like a child's in a backpack
carrier. Then wrote his anthology
piece, began it while she changed the Pamper
full of mustardy shit. Again rage
blisters my wet forehead as the page
stays blank, and you tug my jeans knee, whimper
"I *want* you!" I want you, too. In the child-
sized rowboat in Regent's Park, sick with a man,
and I hadn't spoken to another
grown-up for two days, I played Amazon
Queen and Princess with you. You splashed pond water
outside my fantasy, nineteen months old.

The bathroom tiles are very pink and new.
Out the window, a sixty-foot willow
tree forks, droops. Planted eighteen years ago,
its huge roots choke the drains. The very blue
sky is impenetrable. I hear you
whine outside the locked door. You're going to cry.
If I open the door, I'll slap you. I've
hit you six times this morning. I threw
you on the rug and smacked your bottom. Slapped
your face. Slapped your hands. I sit on the floor.
We're both scared. I picked you up, held you, lov-
ing your cheek's curve. Yelled, shook you. I want to stop
this day. I cringe on the warm pink tiles of
a strange house. We cry on both sides of the door.

Chip took you to your grandmother's today.
You scoop sand-cakes from your orange-and-blue
dump truck, while he reads *The Times Book Review*
on a hot slatted bench four feet away.
Solitary for work, I pay bills, spray
the roaches' climbing party on the flank
of students' dittoed manuscripts and bank
statements. Myself as four-year-old, I play
with your clean clothes, open my closet, finger
old lives' skirts dependent on plastic hangers.
You ask for dresses now, and I demur,
then buy you a crisp shift, blue with white cats,
which I just once have offered you to wear.
I love you most when you are what I'm not.

Up from D.C.

We were six women. My lover
was the youngest. Her cabled shoulders
glistened like her short dark hair.
Tucked, unnoticed, in a sprawling slum
our house was under siege.

We were six women, one
my lover, in a wooden
house, waiting
for the danger
to be over.

In a round tin tub
a woman scrubs
the shape from a baby's
face. The plump brown
child's red hair-ribbon tells: a girl.
Immerses her again, head
under. I cry out, seize her.
You, baby-shaped, face
shapeless, sprawl in a
deck chair. I run, gasping, grab
you too. Is it too late?
Your chins lump like putty.

We looked out a cracked window
on the second floor, from a bare
room: scorched floorplanks, cobwebs.
Dust. Dusty outside,
porched row houses of a Southern slum,
one, cater-corner across, enamelled red.

Coffee cans sprout grapefruit shrubs from pits.
An old black woman in a faded print
dress sits behind them, rocking,
waiting for the danger to be over.

Her sweaty runner's limbs
sprawl across mine, arm on
my shoulder, calf
knotted against my knee. We hunch
below the windowsill, cramped. Still
heat. Roaches run errands.
Her angular
cheekbones glint like blades.
After this, we will not
scavenge. We hope
to survive. The others move
lightly in the hallway. One bald bulb
dangles. One of them
may have given us away.

I try to run with the two
limp puckered babies
grasping my neck, still
chilly and damp, my arms
under their buttocks, their plump
legs slack. Is it too late?

Light squeezes through bamboo slats.
I squeeze my eyes shut. Corduroy
wales pleat my skin through sheets.
You're awake, humming, in the other room,
golden and rosy, blue Grow Pajamas
over scabby knees. In a minute
we will lock on the day's love, the day's rage.
In a minute I will hold you in my arms.

Huge Baby Blues

Written with the letters that can be used in an eight-segment
wiring diagram, to print out poem, letter by letter on L E D dis-
play board: A, B, C, E, F, G, H, I, J, L, N, O, P, S, U, Y.

S O S HUGE BABY LOOSE!
SHE'S FULL OF POISON APPLE JUICE,
SHE'S FULL OF PUNS 'N' LION PISS,
AS NOISY AS CHINESE POLICE.

SHE SAILS ABALONE SHELLS,
SHE SLOPS EGGS IN SCALLION SAUCE.
SHE JOINS GANGS OF YELLING PEOPLE.
SHE SLEEPS IN A USEFUL BUS.

SHE SIPS GIN ON GYPSY SHIPS.
SHE CAN CUSS IN JAPANESE:
"BABOON-BELLY-JELLO-BALLS"
SHE SAYS SEALS CAN SING THESE SONGS

SHE'LL HANG BACON ON PIG'S NOSES.
SHE PLAYS BALL ON FALLING HILLS.
SHE CAN LEAP IN OCEAN POOLS.
SHE CAN LAY ON SUCH A FUSS!

NINE HISPANIC FLYING NUNS
CHOOSE LUNCHS IN A GAY CAFE:
"CHOP SUEY, BAGELS, FISH SOUFFLE,
PAPAYA JUICE, PINEAPPLE FLAN,

SOY SAUCE, YES, OH, COFFEE, PLEASE
I FANCY A BANANA ICE"
SHE CAN PINCH A BUSY CHEF
COY AS ANY CABIN BOY.

LUNCHES, GLASSES, SLIP, FLOP BANG,
SPILLING, SPLASHING, SLIPPING, GLOP!
A BAHFUL CHEF HAVE BOILING BUNS.
FLYING NUNS FLAP, FLY ESCAPE!

HAIL FALLS ON A SLUSHY PLAIN.
SHE IS LONELY AS SLUGGISH
SPANIEL PUPPY IN A PIGPEN.
NO ONE SINGS A SONG IN ENGLISH.

NO ONE SINGS A SONG IN SPANISH.
SHE IS YOUNG AS JANIS JOPLIN'S
CHOICE OF BESSIE'S EPIC BLUES.
SINGING NUNS CAN BE SO CLANNISH.

SUN IS SHINING, FINE AS FOIL,
ON AN OCEAN BILGY BLUE.
OUCH! I FEEL A FISH AS FLIPPY
AS A FELON FLEEING JAIL.

BICYCLING ON SOGGY SPINACH
FEEBLY LEGGY AS A FOAL.
CALL A CAB I HALF AN—NO
I'LL PENSION OFF A FANCY FINISH,

COUGH UP AN ESOPHAGUS
FULL OF GOLDEN ONION SOPU. . .
SHE'S A BILIOUS GENIUS, YES.
IF SHE'S NOISY, SHE'S LESS FUSSY.

SHE IS HIGHLY FALLIBLE.
CAN SHE SPELL? OH NO! A BANG!
GUNS OF GIGGLING JELLY BEANS?
BABBLING ANGELS GO INSANE.

Third Snowfall

"Take with you also my curly-headed four-year-old child."
JOSEPHINE MILES: *"Ten Dreamers in a Motel"*

Another storm, another blizzard
soaks the shanks and chills the gizzard.
Indoors, volumed to try a Stoic,
a four-year-old plays the *Eroica*
three times through. Young Ludwig's ears?
No, only an engineer's
delight in Running the Machine.
Pop! Silence? "I was just seein'
if I could make the tape run back."
"Don't." "If the knob is on 8-track
and I put on a record, what
happens? . . . It's turning, but it's not
playing." "That's what happens." "Oh.
Which dial is for the radio?
I'm going to jump up on your back!
Swing me around!" A subtle *crack*.
and not-so-subtle knives-in-spine.
"Get down, my back's gone out! Don't whine
about it, I'm the one that's hurt."
"I'm sorry . . . Did I have dessert?
What's water made of? Can it melt?"
(I know how Clytemnestra felt.)
"I want a cookie. What is Greek?
Will I be taller by next week?
Is this the way a vampire growls?
I'm going to dress up in the towels.
Look! I can slide on them like skis!
Hey, I've got dried glue on my knees.
Hey, where are people from? The *first*

ones, I mean. What was the Worst
Thing you Ever Ate?" *Past* eight
at last, I see. "Iva, it's late."
"It's not. I want some jam on bread."
"One slice, then get your ass in bed."
"No, wait until my record's over.
I want my doll. And the Land Rover
for Adventure People. Mom, are
you *listening?* Where's the doll's pajamas?
There's glue or something in my hair.
Can I sleep in my underwear?
I think I need the toy fire-fighter
guy too . . . I'm thirsty . . ." *und so weiter.*

Iva's Pantoum

We pace each other for a long time.
I packed my anger with the beef jerky.
You are the baby on the mountain. I am
in a cold stream where I led you.

I packed my anger with the beef jerky.
You are the woman sticking her tongue out
in a cold stream where I led you.
You are the woman with spring water palms.

You are the woman sticking her tongue out.
I am the woman who matches sounds.
You are the woman with spring water palms.
I am the woman who copies.

You are the woman who matches sounds.
You are the woman who makes up words.
You are the woman who copies
her cupped palm with her fist in clay.

I am the woman who makes up words.
You are the woman who shapes
a drinking bowl with her fist in clay.
I am the woman with rocks in her pockets.

I am the woman who shapes.
I was a baby who knew names.
You are the child with rocks in her pockets.
You are the girl in a plaid dress.

You are the woman who knows names.
You are the baby who could fly.
You are the girl in a plaid dress
upside-down on the monkey bars.

You are the baby who could fly
over the moon from a swinging perch
upside-down on the monkey bars.
You are the baby who eats meat.

Over the moon from a swinging perch
the feathery goblin calls her sister.
You are the baby who eats meat
the bitch wolf hunts and chews for you.

The feathery goblin calls her sister:
"You are braver than your mother.
The bitch wolf hunts and chews for you.
What are you whining about now?"

You are braver than your mother
and I am not a timid woman:
what are you whining about now?
My palms itch with slick anger,

and I'm not a timid woman.
You are the woman I can't mention;
my palms itch with slick anger.
You are the heiress of scraped knees.

You are the woman I can't mention
to a woman I want to love.
You are the heiress of scraped knees:
scrub them in mountain water.

To a woman, I want to love
women you could turn into,
scrub them in mountain water,
stroke their astonishing faces.

Women you could turn into
the scare mask of Bad Mother
stroke their astonishing faces
in the silver-scratched sink mirror.

The scare mask of Bad Mother
crumbles to chunked, pinched clay,
sinks in the silver-scratched mirror.
You are the Little Robber Girl, who

crumbles the clay chunks, pinches
her friend, gives her a sharp knife.
You are the Little Robber Girl, who
was any witch's youngest daughter.

Our friend gives you a sharp knife,
shows how the useful blades open.
Was any witch's youngest daughter
golden and bold as you? You run and

show how the useful blades open.
You are the baby on the mountain. I am
golden and bold as you. You run and
we pace each other for a long time.

The Hang-Glider's Daughter

for Catherine Logan

My forty-year-old father learned to fly.
Bat-winged, with a magic marble fear
keeping his toast down, he walks off a sheer
shaved cliff into the morning. On Sunday
mornings he comes for us. Liane and I
feed the baby and Mario, wash up, clear
the kitchen mess. Maman is never there;
that is the morning she and Joseph try
to tell the other pickers how the Word
can save them. Liane gets me good and mad
changing her outfit sixteen times, while I
have to change the baby. All the way
up the hill road she practices on him, flirt-
ing like she does at school. My back teeth hurt

from chewing Pepper Gum on the bad side.
She's three years younger. I'm three years behind.
Did he *mean* that? Shift the gum. Did I remind
Mario, if the baby cries, he needs
burping? I can stretch out on the back seat.
The olive terraces stacked in the sunshine
are shallow stairs a giant child could climb.
My hiking shoes look giant on my feet.
Maman says "a missed boy." What do I miss?
I wonder what the word in English is
for that. Funny, that we should have been born
somewhere we wouldn't even understand
the language now. I was already three
when we left. If someone hypnotized me

would I talk English like a three-year-old?
The bright road twists up; bumpily we shift
gears, breathe deep. In the front pouch of my sweat-
shirt, I've still got my two best marbles. Rolled
in thumb and finger, they click, points gained, told
beads. Not for Joseph's church. If I forgot
French, too, who would I be inside my head?
My hands remember better: how to hold
my penknife to strip branches, where to crack
eggs on a bowl rim, how to pile a block
tower—when I was little—high as my nose.
Could I, still? The box of blocks is Mario's
now. My knee's cramped. I wish that I could walk
to Dad's house, or that I was up front, talk-

ing to him. How does he feel, suddenly slung
from brilliant nylon, levering onto air
currents like a thinking hawk? I'd be scared.
I'd be so scared I can't think it. Maybe a long
slope on my skateboard's like that. Climbing
isn't scary: no time. The air's fizzy, you're care-
ful what rock you hang your weight from, and where
your toes wedge. My calves ache, after, ribs sting,
but I'm good for something. What I like high
is mountains. I'll go up the hill behind
Dad's house this afternoon. I'll pick Liane
flowers. Nahh, we'll be leafing magazines
for school clothes on the sun porch after lunch.
I like those purple bell-spikes. My cleats crunch

the crumble; I stretch to the ledge and pull
out the whole rooted stalk. Sometimes there's twelve
bells, purple as—purple as nothing else

except a flower, ugly and beautiful
at once. Across my face come the two smells:
grandmother's linen-chest spice-sweet petals
and wet dirt clinging, half meat, half metal,
all raw. Between them I smell myself,
sweaty from climbing, but it's a woman's
sweat. I had one of the moon dreams again.
I stood on the flyover facing purple
sea, head up, while a house-huge full moon hurtled
toward me; then it was me flying, feet still
on the road. We're here, on top of the hill.

Occasions

Sonnet Ending with a Film Subtitle

for Judith Landry

Life has its nauseating ironies:
The good die young, as often has been shown;
Chaste spouses catch Venereal Disease;
And feminists sit by the telephone.
Last night was rather bleak, tonight is starker.
I may stare at the wall till half-past-one.
My friends are all convinced Dorothy Parker
Lives, but is not well, in Marylebone.
I wish that I could imitate my betters
And fortify my rhetoric with guns.
Some day we women all will break our fetters
And raise our daughters to be Lesbians.
(I wonder if the bastard kept my letters?)
Here follow untranslatable French puns.

Introductory Lines

written for the Formal Poetry issue of The Little Magazine, *1978*

Rushing to press, it still would seem evasion
not to compose a Verse for this Occasion
to introduce and celebrate our choices
of forms shaped by contemporary voices
(received forms, or invented, or adapted
from Norse, or Anglo-Saxon as one chap did).
At best form gives concinnity, precision,
paring of words and widening of vision,
play for the mind, focus that is self-critical.
Poets, and poems, are not apolitical.
Women and other radicals who choose
venerable vessels for subversive use
affirm what Sophomore Survey often fails
to note: God and Anonymous are not white males.
"We always crafted language just as they did.
We have the use, and we reclaim the credit."

One form perennially apposite,
the useful garment of the sonnet fit
lover, fabulist, feminist, and wit
—those categories not, of course, exclusive.
Concise, ornate, colloquial, allusive
language tidewashed Cathedral Station's floor,
low pun to philosophic metaphor.
A camera on a rotating boom,
six words spin slowly round and pan the room:
I would not like to have to choose between a
sestina on composing a sestina
and one that's a whodunit thirty-nine
lines long—and science fiction has a fine

champion, in sonnet sequence. Bible and fairy,
sexy, perverse, domestic, cautionary
tales are told, some controversy sowed.
There's one syllabic, one Pindaric ode.
There's birth, love, death, work, solitude (no money,
oddly enough). There's quite a lot that's funny,
and everything that's funny is not slight.
Poets who always, poets who seldom write
in forms, well-known or unknown, all responded.
(*Please* don't send whole verse novels, like someone did!)
A Wiccean muse, Form can transform like Circe.

P.S. There are no haiku; that's a mercy.

For Getting Started in a New Place

Invoke the pines, the bushy oak,
the young girl's bed in which you woke
hugging an absent body; call
on: coffee in the dining hall,
three black cups, slice of brown-bran toast,
the Jewish woman fabulist
of gruesome verisimilitudes,
the chunky plates of breakfast foods
for the matutinal colonists.
Invoke your daughter, whom you kissed
and tickled, yelled at, sang to, stroked,
put on a yellow bus; invoke
your mother at cantankerous
senile sixty-eight; her nurse
whose Caribbean histories
people the close Bronx room as she
bridges archipelagoes.
Invoke whatever you can use;
sebaceous pores, querulous gut,
nostalgic genitalia, but
put them to work and shelve your self-
abusive tendencies, a shelf
already stocked with "necessary"
errands that can fill up every
minute you're not asleep, shitting,
or eating. Call on the last unwitting
prophet in Central Park playground.
Call on your mother's bank-account.
Reinflict some remembered pain;
invoke the sun out (*please!*), the rain
away; invoke your appetite
for lunch; pick up a pen and write.

Lines Declining a Transatlantic
Dinner Invitation
for Charlie and Tom

Regretfully, I proffer my excuses.
Number not less than Graces, more than Muses:
Auden's casting call for a dinner party.
He was a genius who was often smart. He
did not think hosts should count their guests in pairs,
unless they had loveseats and no hard chairs.
He was benignly daft for Small Odd Numbers:
a table choked with elbows soon encumbers
wit. I'm sure you'll all be very witty.
I'll miss it, snowed in here in New York City.
But, being *d'un certain age,* we come to know:
better to be discussed than be *de trop.*
The unexpected often is disaster.
If one arrives a month or an hour faster
than looked for, something that one cannot like
might happen: cab drivers would be on strike;
one's friends would be that morning reconciled
with lover, spouse, or adolescent child,
whose tears, A-Levels, or Social Disease
will call them home before the fruit and cheese;
the woman-poet-hating editor
looms ominously near the kitchen door
where a zinc bucket slops up the cold rain
that's sluiced down since the roof fell in again;
one host is wrapped in blankets in the attic: a
damp-inspired episode of his sciatica;
the other, peeling sprouts in a clogged sink,
scowls through a fourth compensatory drink;
somebody else has brought along a new

chum who was scathing in *The New Review;*
there'd be the flight to Amsterdam at nine;
simply, there might be insufficient wine.
As passports take two weeks to put in shape,
this all may have a flavor of sour grape.
Speaking of grapes—I hope you bought *Biscuit—*
pour one more brandy, as it were, on me.

Iva's Birthday Poem

All horns should honk like anything!
All taxicabs should come alive
and stand on their back wheels and sing
that Iva Alyxander's five!

The fish are burbling in the lake,
the bees are buzzing in their hive,
the candles flicker on the cake
that Iva Alyxander's five!

She's put on inches, weight, and speed.
Who knows what wonders may arrive.
I prophesy she'll learn to read,
now Iva Alyxander's five.

Dolphins leap in the swimming pool
to watch her famous cartwheel dive.
Jump! Flip! Swirl! Splash! *Extremely* cool,
now Iva Alyxander's five.

She'll hire a plane—she has a plan—
and teach her mother how to drive.
She can, if anybody can,
now Iva Alyxander's five.

She's smart, she's tough, you've got to hand her
that—so praise in prose and verse
the newly five-year-old Commander
(In Training) of the Whole Universe.

The Acrobats, the Metropoli-
tan Opera and the Royal Ballet
will jointly stage a birthday gala,
for you-know-who is five today!

Wonder Woman and Superman
and Robot Warriors from Mars
all pick up rainbow spray-paint cans
and write her name on subway cars.

They hand out ice cream in the station
with chocolate bars as big as bricks.
There won't be such a celebration
till Iva Alyxander's Six!

We'll toast her health! So pour a drink of
champagne, or chocolate soda! I've
the greatest daughter I can think of
and Iva Alyxander's FIVE ! ! ! ! !

July 19, 1979

I'll write a sonnet just to get in form,
allowing fifteen minutes by the clock
to build gratuitously block by block
of quatrains. Almost six, pale sunlight, warm
(last night we thought there'd be a thunderstorm).
The crickets fiddle buzz-saws without vowels.
I've had thrice-daily bouts of runny bowels,
which seems, on travels south, to be the norm.
I must avoid the self-indulgent stance
of lovesick troubadours—that isn't wise,
in spite of being in the South of France
with a capricious woman whose blue eyes
invest the genre with some relevance.
She says they're green. I've done my exercise.

Partial Analysis
(of the "Giudizio Universale" of Giovanni di Paolo)
for Richard Howard

Do you imagine, wakeful late in bed,
a Gay Bar Paradiso, inlaid gold,
or are you inexplicably impelled
to Hell, where naked people eat boiled toad?

Beneath six trees in fruit with golden apples,
two boys are stroked by a greybeard schoolmaster.
A Carmelite comes up behind her sister
(praying) and smooths her cowl and cups her nipples.

A monk is taking off another monk's
belt. Two svelte blonde maidens, looking rapt,
caress each other's breasts. Pink incorrupt-
ible chubby martyred Innocents give thanks.

A nun, an Arab, and a bearded priest
exchange a blessing that goes round three ways.
Three angels have three monks down on their knees.
A cardinal greets a youth with a slim waist

cinctured in red. In Hell, it's very dark
and pasty-looking people with no clothes
are pinched and pushed and boiled in noxious baths
—it's not unlike some places in New York—

while everyone looks put-upon or bored.
But everyone looks Interestingly Bad
in Heaven, their reward for being good:
Hesperidean light, and no holds barred.

Tranche Romancière

"Franchement, je m'en fiche de la vertu!"
said Maud, letting her supple haunches sink
into the velvet armchair. "I can count
on the fingers of a defective hand
women with firm ideas on how to act
who behave themselves, by *my* standards, well!"

"No good dripping like a bucket from the Well
of Loneliness, as if there were intrinsic virtue
in taste or distaste for a harmless act.
They'll plumb the depths of gloom that they can sink
to, all unconscious, on the other hand,
of things they do for which they are account-

able." "You're such a moralist!" the Count-
ess said. "If I didn't know you so well,
I never would imagine you could hand-
le ambiguities so brusquely. Virtue
is not, speaking abstractly, like that sink-
ing in melted chocolate feeling. Act

your age. Or mine. My great-grand-aunt the act-
ress was forgiven for her bank-account.
She started with her elbows in the sink.
Not that she did it, but that she did it well
is where you or I would locate the virtue."
She weighed a green fig in her cool cupped hand.

When she was twenty-five she had been hand-
some; thirty years in the field of act-

ion (as she called it) had had the virtue
(Maud thought) of refinement, count-
ing times her tall friend had been all-too-well
acclaimed. She spoke, making her voice sink

to philosophic alto. "We must synch-
ronize words to images. I hand
the palm to cinéastes; they make a well-
fleshed metaphor." "That kind of act
exceeds the act of kind." "Dear, I can count
on your wit; sobriety's *not* your virtue."

"I've other virtues." Standing near the sink,
the Countess pulled five rings off her right hand.
"Actually, I don't feel entirely well . . ."

La Fontaine de Vaucluse

Conte

(Cinderella, sometime after the affair of the glass/fur slipper)

First of all, I'm bored. It's not
what you'd think. Every day, meetings
I can't attend. I sit and sit and stick
my fingers with petit-point needles. Ladies
ignore me, or tell me all their petty secrets
(petty because *they* can't attend meetings)
about this man or that. Even his mistress
—*you* would have assumed he had a mistress—
gritted her teeth and had me come to lunch
and whined about the way she was mistreated.
And I suppose she's right, she was mistreated.
The plumbing is appalling, but I won't
go into that. He is forever brooding
on lost choices he might have made; before
three days had passed, I'd heard, midnight to dawn,
about the solitary life he craved.
Why not throw it all up, live on the coast
and fish, no, no, impossible with wives!
Why *not* throw it all up, live on the coast,
or cut my hair, teach (what?) little girls
and live at home with you? I schooled myself
for this, despised *you* for going to meetings,
reading instead of scrubbing, getting fat
(scorn of someone who burns off bread and puddings).
I made enduring tedium my virtue.
I'll have to keep my virtue. I could envy
you, but I'm sick of envy. Please allow
me now, at least, to call you sisters. Yours, C.

Why We Are Going Back to Paradise Island

He has just cornered and skewered
a rat with a broomstick. He once shot
a milk doe, sloppily and badly.
He let his cousin's kitten starve, to show him.
Stalking at dawn in March, when he was twelve,
he shot his small brother by mistake.

He mourns his son dead twelve hours old,
his father gulping in an oxygen
tent, the brother whose surprised
gasp explodes his waking lips again.
He hunts them down in dreams. His fat smart
baby daughter wanders in front of a truck

so he buys an identical pickup truck
and picks up another older little daughter
aged, say, eight, and drives her out to the woods
behind the motel, and bashes her when she screams.
Does he, really? He imagines
the wind, the smell of mouldy birch leaves

and blown smoke. What if he really hated
his wife, if she were nothing but a cunt
and her cunt were a swamp lined with razor-blades?
He has two wives, really. One lives on pills.
He pays her therapist. The other has
her ribs taped where he got her with a two-by-four.

Numinous and glowing, stained-glass windows,
poems crafted and spare as winter birch,

he imagines the rapist, the voyeur,
the child-murderer, the telephonist
whispering threats in the night. He imagines
hiring someone to do it to his wife

while she screams and pisses herself. No, while
she groans with delight. She takes it in her
mouth, glistening black, twice as big as his.
Would a sheep's hole feel the same, or the cold
tight gap of a beached dog-shark, last gasps
coming together, before limp flesh?

He was not the enemy. He was the hurt
idealist, poet, he read the books
you did. His manners were better than mine.
You wanted him to praise you and make you real.
I wanted to hear about his childhood.
We wanted him to love us.

Visiting Chaldon Down

for Jeanne Wordsworth

We left the Volvo in a cleft of grave-
barrows. The road ran out, ran down
to tractor- and pony-gouged mud. Green hills
slid from lip to cup-bowl. The heat-
meniscus lidded and lensed us, swallowed
our sounds. Not March except for harsh
plant smells; then, beyond hills, the raw sea.
Two men, two women: they, thirty years friends;
we, recent strangers. My sometime lover
in a patched tweed jacket, heard, probably
not for the first time, your sometime husband
(vast glasses and a pea jacket, peppered
hair over the collar) juxtapose
Romans on Powys and his brace of Yankee
wives. One had Chidioch farmhouse, one
the garden shed. You thrust wide fists down
in sandy cardigan pockets, scuffed
mud, worried by the irrational
like a big pup's leather bone. You muffled
your angles in orphan clothes. Six years younger than
everyone, Levi's, green corduroy,
I faked bold, not even on approval.
I wanted to wander away, clamber the hills
as usual, wanting (as usual)
to incise his hand on me (it wasn't)
with bright air, mint wind, on chalk
cliff-face with the dead poets, already told
to gorse and cowshit, huddled scrub and stones.
What stones did you grasp and shy
in your own head, on approval in the narrow

smoky kitchen with the lodger's wooden ladder
guiding her platform wedgies down, your own
two daughters, plumpish and pasty, shy
of your shying some unanswerable
through antemenarchal calm? My own
daughter was across the ocean we climbed to.
What can a woman say to another woman,
almost a stranger, toeholding through
an invisible war? I said almost
nothing, held back and held your hand
when your sandal skidded.
                              Dear Jeanne, believe
under all probable beliefs this is
for you. Edna Millay, foreign as I, once walked
across the Downs to cheer that sick man, wrote
one of the stories, without the women. I
read it today: Chaldon Down, Bat's Head; thought
of you. In a bony cove, bottle-green
threaded gravel a white drop down. I sprawled
between two men, on a pebbled spit
jutting sheer lucidity, shying
pebbles, with you wedged in my mind,
reasonably terrified, landlocked behind
us in the muddy pasture.
                              (Reasonably
terrified in the prison of unreason-
able women, you turn and turn a matchbox
over, label-side, wooden-side, on your palm:
the pictured purple flame is numinous;
what is its name?)
                              Over fried eggs
congealing toward thick white-bread toast, across
formica, steam from mugs of weak tea,

I asked if it hurt. We need words
for pain's phyla: cracked ribs, the murderess' next
moment, the birth-work, death snapping
the fan of possibilities
shut, the mind seeded or winged
with uninvited energies. "Sometimes
it fills me with force and joy. The terror
is where it will leave me." Misremembered,
your ripe voice is hybrid. You
were foreign too.

Ordinary Women I

I am the woman you see in Blooming-
dale's ruffling the rack of children's sweaters
on sale, trying on tweed slacks in Better
Sportswear, which I won't buy, browsing and homing
in on unmatched striped sheets on January
Clearance. Rapt with textures, women escalate
leisurely. This is our protectorate.
Our brown or pink skins flush over furry
or frayed coats in smoothing taupe light. We do
not shuffle aside for the man, who is
not here, who built this shelter, our consuming
career. What I am saying to you is
I am the woman you will see blooming
up from our terror, with women: me, you.

Ordinary Women II
for June Jordan and Sara Miles

Mrs. Velez of the Tenants' Association
zig-zags her top-heavy shopping cart through
the usual palette of dogshit, brick-red
to black on grimy leftover snow.
Tenement roofs' stone scrollwork
soot-chiaroscuro on the almost-equinoctial
sky. Old Mrs. Cohen, who still wears a marriage wig,
stiff-legs the stood with Food City-bagged garbage.
Slashed bags everywhere spill chicken bones,
orange peels, crushed milk cartons, piss-soaked
Pampers, broken toys.
Sweat-cracked loafers, runover orange work shoes,
    silver-painted
platform shoes, running-stripe sneakers, a cast on one foot
and newspaper-stuffed single shoe, electric-blue-patent-
    leather-
style-fake-yellow-snakeskin-trim shoes, stand,
pace,
shuffle,
Bop a little,
in front of the liquor store; the hands man brown-bagged
    Ripple.
She has a daughter named Tequila,
little and black and wiry and so is she,
her name's Joanne.
Yellow-trousered Tequila, rising three,
dashes from the separator to the laundry scales,
past two broken dryers.
Sometimes she plays with Iva on the slide.
"I'm OK, I'm goin' to night school, studying
bookkeeping,

but I gotta leave Tequila with my brother—
that's him."
He must be nine,
little and black and wiry, leafs
Spiderman, The Incredible Hulk beside him
on the bracketed row of plastic chairs.
Tequila's run outside.
"Joseph, go *get* her!" He does.
Joanne has a textbook, *American History,*
all-sized thumb-smudges on the library
binding. She has me write my name and number
on a creased notebook-leaf shoved inside.
"What you doin', Tequila? Stay by me, you hear!"
I feel my old brown sheepskin's London label,
my red wool ERA cap . . . Joseph herds
Tequila toward the thrumming washing-
machines. She
scooters a canvas basket to the porthole.
Her left blue Flintstones sneaker is untied.
Tile walls sweat steam and soap. Compact Anne Desirée,
the proprietaire, has my laundry folded
into the Macy's shopping bag. "Comment ça va?"
"Très bien, merci." "Et ta fille?" "Grandissante,
a l'école au moment. Merci bien, au revoir. Bye,
Joanne, Joseph, Tequila!"
Threadbare brown corduroy coat, Army Surplus safari jacket,
orphaned suit coat, raddled blue anorak, black leather
    bomber jacket,
pastel polyester plaid with calf-length back-split skirts,
elbow outside the liquor store;
the hands man brown-bagged Ripple.
The woman who stands on street corners stands
on the street corner, her coffee-bean

264

skin ashy, her plump face Thorazine
swollen. Thin grey coat gaps open
on short white housedress gapped open
on bolstered brown knock knees.
Fragile flesh puffs sink her huge wet eyes,
not looking across the street, or down the street,
not looking at the sidewalk or the sky.

Shirland Road

for Yvonne

This is the other story. There are three
women in a room. Fat glasses, tea-
pot not cleared away, we draw up tides
of talk that clear the beaches and subside
to amicable silence; sip, smoke, lean
back into notebooks, newspapers. The green
unfabled garden darkens. One of the cats
thumps in the window, rumbles on a mat-
ted cushion near the red bars of the fire.
Beyond the magic circle of desire
where shadows stall in storied attitudes,
this continues happening. Warmed blood
unclenches toes and fingers, which can stroke
cat, cushion, massed black hair tangled with smoke
and rosewater. You have strewn second-hand
treasures on all your surfaces, that find,
question, dismiss the eye; buff, blue, brown things
I like. Have we been quiet for a long
time? Vermouth, Eleanor of Aquitaine.
A red moth skitters on the windowpane.
Brown flowers glow on globed light above strewn books.
Marie is writing, too. You've gone to cook
supper: brown garlic, slice a cucumber.
I track my nose into the kitchen, stir
up salad dressing, filch a corner of cheese,
teetering on a balance bridging these
planks of resignation and repose.

La Fontaine de Vaucluse

for Marie Ponsot

"*Why write unless you praise the sacred places . . . ?*"
RICHARD HOWARD: "*Audiences*"

1

Azure striation swirls beyond the stones
flung in by French papas and German boys.
The radio-guide emits trilingual noise.
"Always 'two ladies alone'; we were not alone."
Source, cunt, umbilicus, resilient blue
springs where the sheer gorge spreads wooded, mossed
   thighs:
unsounded female depth in a child-sized
pool boys throw rocks at. Hobbled in platform shoes,
girls stare from the edge. We came for the day
on a hot bus from Avignon. A Swed-
ish child hurls a chalk boulder; a tall girl,
his sister, twelve, tanned, crouches to finger shell-
whorls bedded in rock-moss. We find our way
here when we can; we take away what we need.

2

Here, when we can, we take away what we need:
stones, jars of herb-leaves, scrap-patch workbags stored
in the haphazard rooms we can afford.
Marie and I are lucky: we can feed
our children and ourselves on what we earn.
One left the man who beat her, left hostages
two daughters; one weighs her life to her wages,
finds both wanting and, bought out, stays put, scorn-
ful of herself for not deserving more.

The concierge at Le Régent is forty-six;
there fifteen years, widowed for one, behind
counters a dun perpetual presence, fixed
in sallow non-age till Marie talked to her.
I learn she is coeval with my friends.

            3
I learn she is coeval with my friends:
the novelist of seventy who gives
us tea and cakes; the sister with whom she lives
a dialogue; the old Hungarian
countess' potter daughter, British, dyke,
bravely espoused in a medieval hill
town in Provence; Jane whom I probably will
never know and would probably never like;
Liliane the weaver; Liliane's daughter
the weaver; Liliane's housewifely other
daughter, mothering; the great-grandmother
who drove us through gnarled lanes at Avignon;
the virgin at the source with wedgies on;
Iva, who will want to know what I brought her.

            4
Iva, who will want to know what I brought her
(from Selfridge's, a double-decker bus,
a taxi, Lego; a dark blue flowered dress
from Uniprix; a wickerwork doll's chair
from the Vence market; books; a wrapped-yarn deer;
a batik: girl guitarist who composes
sea creatures, one of three I chose,
two by the pupil, one by the woman who taught her),
might plunge her arms to the elbows, might shy stones,
might stay shy. I'll see her in ten days.

Sometimes she still swims at my center; sometimes
she is a four-year-old an ocean away
and I am on vertiginous terrain
where I am nobody's mother and nobody's daughter.

                5
"Where I am, nobody's mother and nobody's daughter
can find me," words of a woman in pain
or self-blame, obsessed with an absent or present man,
blindfolded, crossing two swords, her back to the water.
The truth is, I wake up with lust and loss
and only half believe in something better;
the truth is that I still write twelve-page letters
and blame my acne and my flabby ass
that I am thirty-five and celibate.
Women are lustful and fickle and all alike,
say the hand-laid flower-pressed sheets at the papermill.
I pay attention to what lies they tell
us here, but at the flowered lip, hesitate,
one of the tamed girls stopped at the edge to look.

                6
One of the tamed girls stopped at the edge to look
at her self in the water, genital self that stains
and stinks, that is synonymous with drains,
wounds, pettiness, stupidity, rebuke.
The pool creates itself, cleansed, puissant, deep
as magma, maker, genetrix. Marie
and I, each with a notebook on her knee,
begin to write, homage the source calls up
or force we find here. There is another source
consecrate in the pool we perch above:
our own intelligent accord that brings

us to the lucid power of the spring
to work at re-inventing work and love.
We may be learning how to tell the truth.

      7
We may be learning how to tell the truth.
Distracted by a cinematic sky,
Paris below two dozen shades of grey,
in borrowed rooms we couldn't afford, we both
work over words till we can tell ourselves
what we saw. I get up at eight, go down
to buy fresh croissants, put a saucepan on
and brew first shared coffee. The water solves
itself, salves us. Sideways, hugging the bank,
two stocky women helped each other, drank
from leathery cupped palms. We make our own
descent downstream, getting our shoes wet, care-
fully hoist cold handsful from a crevice where
azure striation swirls beyond the stones.

Peterborough

Another story still: a porch with trees
—maple and oak, sharpening younger shoots
against the screen; privileged solitude
with early sunlight pouring in a thin
wash on flat leaves like milk on a child's chin.
Light shifts and dulls. I want to love a woman
with my radical skin, reactionary im-
agination. My body is cored with hunger;
my mind is gnarled in oily knots of anger
that push back words: inelegant defeat
of female aspiration. First we're taught
men's love is what we cannot do without;
obliged to do without precisely that:
too fat, too smart, too loud, too shy, too old.
Unloved and underpaid, tonight untold
women will click our failings off, each bead
inflating to a bathysphere, our need
encapsulated in a metal skin,
which we, subaqueous monsters, cannot in-
filtrate. The middle of the road is noon.
Reactive creature with inconstant moon-
tides (no doubt amendable as near-
sightedness, but sacred to How Things Are)
my blood came down and I swarmed up a tree,
intoxicated with maturity.
Woman? Well, maybe—but I was a Grown-
Up, entitled to make up my own
mind, manners, morals, myths—menses small price
to pay for midnight and my own advice.
By next September, something was revenged

on me. Muffled in sweat-soaked wool, I lunged
out of seventh-grade science lab, just quick
enough to get to the Girls' Room and be sick.
Blotched cheeks sucked to my teeth, intestines turn-
ing themselves out, hunched over a churn-
ing womb fisting itself, not quite thirteen,
my green age turned me regularly green.
Our Jewish man G.P. to whom I carried
myself hinted sex helped, once you were married.
Those weren't days I fancied getting laid.
Feet pillowed up, belly on heating pad,
head lolled toward Russian novel on the floor,
I served my time each hour of the four
days of the week of the month for the next ten
years, during which I fucked a dozen men,
not therapeutically, and just as well.
Married to boot, each month still hurt like hell.
The sky thickens, seeps rain. I retrospective-
ly add my annals to our tribe's collective
Book of Passage Rites, and do not say
a woman gave notebook leaves to me today
whose argument was what I knew: desire,
and all the old excuses ranked, conspired:
avoid, misunderstand, procrastinate;
say you're monogamous, or celibate,
sex is too messy, better to be friends
(thirsty for draughts of amity beyond
this hesitation, which has less to do
with her than my quixotic body's too
pertinacious—*tua tam pertinax*
valetudo, neither forward nor back-
ward—malingering, I ask, or healing).
I like her: smart, strong, sane, companionate.

I still love a man: true, but irrelevant.
Then, unavoidably, why not?
She was gone (of course) by this time; I sat
mirrored, eye-to-eye, cornered between
two scalp-high windows framing persistent rain.

Moon Animation

Someone left the keys in that bronze antique
two-seater. The border's not unthinkably far.
We've been sleeping together for a week.
Nothing is impossible anymore.

On the wooded road, our two lean shadows stretch
morning-long in a triple-bill spectacular
moonrise. You tell tall tales of the bowling witch.
Nothing is impossible anymore.

Graveyard moonlight, insufficiently grave
to ground me. I may just swim twenty-four
laps tomorrow. In your lap's one nice place.
Nothing is impossible anymore.

Big as an incandescent volleyball,
the swelled globe drifts to zenith. I explore
your cheek, neck, shoulder, anything at all.
Nothing is impossible anymore.

With shuddering strokes, we offer the full moon
to each other. My hand sinks to the wet core
of your heat and our nerves fugue on a twinned tune.
Nothing is impossible anymore.

Home, and I've

Covered the flowered linen
where I graze
on a convolvulus that hides in
lion grass, and ride in-

to the sunrise on a sand
horse. These days
shorten, but the afternoon simmered
me down. I had dinner

alone, with retrospective
on the blaz-
on of your throat's tiger-lily flush
and your salt sap enough

company until tomorrow.
The fat blue
lamp spills on a ziggurat of books,
mug the same cobalt. Looks

like reprise of lesson one
in how to
keep on keeping on. Easier, with
you fixed hours away; both

solitude and company
have a new
savor: yours. Sweet woman, I'll woman-
fully word a nomen-

clature for what we're doing
when we come
to; come to each other with our eyes,
ears, arms, minds, everything wide

open. Your tonic augments
my humdrum
incantations till they work. I can
stop envying the man

whose berth's the lap where I'd like
to roll home
tonight. I've got May's new book for bed,
steak, greens, and wine inside

me, you back tomorrow, some
words, some laz-
y time (prune the plants, hear Mozart) to
indulge in missing you.

Five Meals

"A table means does it not my dear it means a whole steadiness"

GERTRUDE STEIN: *Tender Buttons*

Slices of ham, pâté, sausage, on lettuce leaves;
cauliflower, wedge of duck in a browned wine
sauce; lettuce, raw cabbage, vinegar and oil;
a square of walnut cake with mocha frosting;
Camembert in green foil, a hard roll, butter;
a half-bottle of champagne, black coffee.

Croissants, butter, orange juice, coffee.
Beaujolais versus St. Emilion. Bibb leaves
with grated sheep's cheese; snails in garlic butter;
roast suckling pig crackling in juice; red wine
in a glass pitcher; chocolate mousse. Breath frosting
the glass in your hand. Brandy in bed. Oil

cost a lot, in huge bottles. Without oil
we ate endive, goat cheese. No coffee
take-outs in Paris. The crème fraîche, peaked like frosting,
you scooped up with moon-green feather-shaped leaves
cross-legged on the bed. We uncorked wine
with my Swiss knife. Between sour cream and butter:

I lick fingers of cream. The gold-foiled butter
cube you've shaped, between jam labels, in oil
crayons. Tongues are smoothed by rough young red wine.
The drawing's edge is a brown stream of coffee.
You save one tangerine with two long leaves
curling the globe. Dark chocolate, like torte frosting

out of the bowl. Morning, cold rain frosting
the cubed panes. Croissants, tartines and butter.
We're still sleepy, but neither of us leaves
a crust. I stroke your peach-furred cheek; hot oil
wells from the source as the first milky coffee
pours down. You have no crayons for the wine

colors. We could only drink white wine
but it's too cold. The rain puddles are frosting
over. We plan excursions with more coffee.
You fold the currant jelly and the butter
labels. In Florence there'll be olive oil
cheap, in baroque tins. Our train leaves

at seven. I leave our New Year's wine
frosting in the kitchen. Rainbows of oil
swirl on warm smells: buttered fresh bread, strong coffee.

Pantoum

There is a serviceable wooden dory
rocking gently at the lip of ocean,
from where her moorline loops back loosely
to an outrider of the wet forest.

Rocking gently at the lip of ocean,
whorled and rosy carapaces glimmer.
To an outrider of the wet forest
who kneels at the undulant flat belly

whorled and rosy carapaces glimmer
under, the water is a mirror dreaming.
Who kneels at the undulant flat belly
feels her pulse gyre in the liquid circles.

Under the water is a mirror dreaming
furled leaves. She kneads and presses her friend's spine,
feels her pulse gyre in the liquid circles
her palm oils on smooth skin, opening like

furled leaves. She kneads and presses her friend's spine,
enters her own blood's tiderush, leaves
her palm oils on smooth skin. Opening like
shrubbery parting to bare fingers, she

enters. Her own blood's tiderush leaves
her charged with flammable air, igniting the
shrubbery. Parting to bare fingers, she
grows, reaches into the fire licking

her, charged with flammable air, igniting the
dry tinder, and the wet places that flame like brandy.
Grows, reaches into the fire licking
her clean, that nourishes as it consumes

dry tinder. And the wet places that flame like brandy
are knowledgeable. They affirm
her: clean. That nourishes as it consumes
detritus of self-doubt, whispers she fears

are knowledgeable. They affirm
each other in themselves. Still, when the
detritus of self-doubt whispers, she fears
the empty pool, that secret. They could lose

each other in themselves, still. When the
postcards begin arriving, they depict
the empty pool, that secret. They could lose
jobs, balance, money, central words, music.

Postcards begin arriving. They depict
themselves living in a perfect landscape, with
jobs, balance, money: central. Words, music
one made for the other, late at night, as they rocked

themselves. Living in a perfect landscape, with
passionate friends, you'd ache, she thinks.
One made for the other? Late at night, as they rocked
into incognate languages, were they still

passionate friends? You'd ache, she thinks,
if your mind buzzed with translations of denial
into incognate languages. Were they still
anywhere near the hidden rainforest?

If your mind buzzed with translations of denial,
you might not see the gapping in the hedgerows,
anywhere near the hidden rainforest,
a child could push through, or a tall woman stooping.

You might not see the gapping in the hedgerows
at first. She grew up here, points out where
a child could push through, or a tall woman. Stooping,
howevermany shoulder in, to the brambles

at first. She grew up here, points out where
the path mounts, damp under eye-high ferns.
However many shoulder into the brambles,
each one inhales the solitude of climbing.

The path mounts, damp under eye-high ferns.
Cedars aspire to vanishing point in the sky.
Each one inhales the solitude of climbing
lichenous rocks. In soft perpetual rain,

cedars aspire to vanishing point in the sky,
then, sea-stained and enormous, niched for foothold,
lichenous rocks, in soft perpetual rain.
Each, agile or clumsy, silently scales them.

Then, see: Stained and enormous, niched for foothold
by tidepools sloshing broken shells and driftwood
(each, agile or clumsy, silently scales them
to her own size), boulders embrace the Sound.

By tidepools sloshing broken shells, and driftwood
from where her moorline loops back loosely
to her own sides (boulders embrace the sound
there) is a serviceable wooden dory.

From Provence

At the Régence, I wonder, is the brain
fed by the eye, or does it feed the eye?
On the red tabletop, sunlit, my glass,
half-full, releases fizz into the air.
Two women at the next table look like
Park Slope dykes. Or are they speaking French?

(Some Park Slope dykes speak perfectly good French,
but wouldn't, here.) I do have dykes on the brain.
"I never met a woman I wouldn't like,"
said Natalie Barney, catching the green eye
of the teen-aged Polish painter in an air-
man's casque of matching green lamé. Her glass

of pear-colored pastis crackling on *glace
pilée* (as it was happening in French)
stood precisely between them. The night air
was laced with lavender. I think the brain
informs the genitals of what the eye
suspects. "I'm never certain if I'd like

to do what I think with somebody I like,"
said the girl, who is transforming in the glass
of fiction what I might have said if I
were approached by Natalie Barney, speaking French,
as I'd have to, to say to those women (Brain-
storm for something plausible), "The air

smells of the sea this morning. You've an *air
sympat'*, and though it's bold of me, I'd like

282

to know you." But habit exiles the brain,
reactionary anarchist, with glass
a foot thick between thought and action. French-
women wear short hair, but not plaid shirts, and eye

makeup is a giveway. Now I
actually *need* a light. With the air
of a habituée, one reads a French
newspaper. The other, who does look like
someone I know, stands up, empties her glass
of orange juice. The young Pole was a Brain

at school. Brains counted but (she squinted) eyes
are seen while seeing, not like one-way glass.
The Frenchwomen have vanished in thin air!

Canzone

Consider the three functions of the tongue:
taste, speech, the telegraphy of pleasure,
are not confused in any human tongue;
yet, sinewy and singular, the tongue
accomplishes what, perhaps, no other organ
can. Were I to speak of giving tongue,
you'd think two things at least; and a cooked tongue,
sliced, on a plate, with caper sauce, which I give
my guest for lunch, is one more, to which she'd give
the careful concentration of her tongue
twice over, to appreciate the taste
and to express—it would be in good taste—

a gastronomic memory the taste
called to mind, and mind brought back to tongue.
There is a paucity of words for taste:
sweet, sour, bitter, salty. Any taste,
however multiplicitous its pleasure,
complex its execution (I might taste
that sauce ten times in cooking, change its taste
with herbal subtleties, chromatic organ
tones of clove and basil, good with organ
meats) must be described with those few taste-
words, or with metaphors, to give
my version of sensations it would give

a neophyte, deciding whether to give
it a try. She might develop a taste.
(You try things once; I think you have to give
two chances, though, to know your mind, or give

up on novelties.) Your mother tongue
nurtures, has the subtleties which give
flavor to words, and words to flavor, give
the by no means subsidiary pleasure
of being able to describe a pleasure
and recreate it. Making words, we give
the private contemplations of each organ
to the others, and to others, organ-

ize sensations into thoughts. Sentient organ-
isms, we symbolize feeling, give
the spectrum (that's a symbol) each sense organ
perceives, by analogy, to others. Disorgan-
ization of the senses is an acquired taste
we all acquire; as speaking beasts, it's organ-
ic to our discourse. The first organ
of acknowledged communion is the tongue
(tripartite diplomat, which after tongu-
ing a less voluble expressive organ
to wordless efflorescences of pleasure
offers up words to reaffirm the pleasure).

That's a primary difficulty: pleasure
means something, and something different, for each organ;
each person, too. I may take exquisite pleasure
in boiled eel, or blancmange—or not. One pleasure
of language is making known what not to give.
And think of a bar of lavender soap, a pleasure
to see and, moistened, rub on your skin, a pleasure
especially to smell, but if you taste
it (though smell is most akin to taste)
what you experience will not be pleasure;
you almost retch, grimace, stick out your tongue,
slosh rinses of ice water over your tongue.

But I would rather think about your tongue
experiencing and transmitting pleasure
to one or another multi-sensual organ
—like memory. Whoever wants to give
only one meaning to that, has untutored taste.

Taking Notice

Taking Notice

"two women together is a work
nothing in civilization has made simple"
ADRIENNE RICH: XXI *Love Poems*

I

My child wants dolls, a tutu, that girls' world made
pretty and facile. Sometimes. Sometimes I
want you around uncomplicatedly.
Work every day; love (the same one) every
night: old songs and new choir the parade
of coupled women whose fidelity
is a dyke icon. You are right: if we
came to new love and friendship with a sad
baggage of endings, we would come in bad
faith, and bring, rooted already, seed
of a splitting. Serial monogamy
is a cogwheeled hurt, though you don't like the word.
The neighbor's tireless radio sings lies
through the thin wall behind my desk and bed.

2

Morning: the phone jangles me from words: you,
working at his place, where you slept last night,
missed me. You'll bring drawings. I missed you too.
What centers, palpably swelling my tight
chest: lust, tenderness, an itch of tears.
Three Swedish Ivy rootlings get a pot.
Wash earth-crumbed hands, strip, put long underwear
on, tug, zip, buckle, tie, button, go out—
a mailbox full of bills and circulars.
I trust you: it's a knife-edge of surprise
through words I couldn't write down, subvocalize
across Eighty-First Street, cold as it was

at eight when I put Iva on the bus,
stalling through iced slush between frost-rimed cars.

3

When that jackbooted choreography
sends hobnailed cabrioles across a brain,
the stroked iron pulling lovers together pulls
them apart. Through the ecstatic reverie
of hands, eyes, mouths, our surfaces' silken
sparking, heraldic plants and animals
alive on our tender cartography,
the homesick victim glimpses the coast of pain,
hears the familiar argot of denial.
Woman I love, as old, as new to me
as any moment of delight risked in
my lumpy heretofore unbeautiful
skin, if I lost myself in you I'd be
no better lost than any other woman.

4

She twists scraps of her hair in unshelled snails
crossed by two hairpins. It takes forty-five
minutes. I'm twelve. I've come in to pee. I've
left *Amazing Stories* and *Weird Tales*
in the hamper. "Don't believe what you read.
Women who let men use them are worse than
whores. Men despise them. I can understand
prostitutes, never 'free love.'" Not freed
to tell her what I thought of *More Than Human*,
I wipe between my mottled oversized
girl-haunches. I'll be one of the despised,
I know, as she forbids with her woman's
body, flaccid, gaunt in a greyed nightgown,
something more culpable for us than "men."

5

"I never will be only a Lesbian."
Bare rubber, wedged beside its tube of cream
in the bookshelf near your bed, your diaphragm
lies on Jane Cooper's poem and Gertrude Stein.
I've torn our warm cocoon again. I listen.
Our sweatered breasts nuzzle under the quilt.
(Yes, there's one in my bathroom cabinet;
unused, now.) If a man sleeps with men, and women,
he's *queer: vide* Wilde, Goodman, Gide, Verlaine.
A woman who does can be "passionately
heterosexual" (said Norman Pearson of H. D.).
Anyone's love with women doesn't count.
Rhetoric, this. You talk about your friend.
I hold you, wanting whatever I want.

6

Angry, I speak, and pass the hurt to you,
your pencil-smudged face naked like a child's.
Each time we don't know what we're getting into
or out of. Later, washed out and reconciled,
we wait on the subway platform, Mutt and Jeff
puffed out with football socks and Duofolds,
word-shy, habitually bold enough
to sit thigh against corduroy thigh and hold
hands; though, ungendered in thick winter gear,
only your cheeks' epicene ivory
makes us the same sex. No one looks healthy
in the perpetual fluorescence. Here
(you say) the light is the same night and day,
but it feels like night at night anyway.

7

If we talk, we're too tired to make love; if we
make love, these days, there's hardly time to talk.
We sit to share supper once, twice a week.
You're red and white with cold; we're brusque, scared, shy.
Difficult speech curdles the café au lait
next morning. In the short twelve hours between
we rubbed, laughed, tongued, exhorted, listened, came,
slept like packed spoons. Wrapped up against the day
we trudge through slush as far as the downtown
subway, brush cold-tattered lips. You're gone
to hunch sock-shod over your camera, while
I stare a spiral notebook down six miles
north, indulging some rich weave of weeks where
we'd work, play, not cross-reference calendars.

8

The sitter, sniffling, leaves, clicks the door shut.
Shuck boots; back from Womanbooks. Iva fights
the quilt in her top bunk, in striped underwear.
A painter read from six months journals, through
learning she loved a woman, at forty-two.
If you were here, we'd compare pasts, compare
process to language, art; you're not, tonight.
Back at the revolution all is not
well. We, women, patient mockers of our own
enterprise, are mined with self-destruction.
We build what we need. We wreck what we build.
I'm making coffee when the telephone
rings: you, ducked into a booth across town?
Another woman, friend, as risked, as real.

9

In my boots and blazer I feel like Julien Sorel.
Should I bow from the waist, flourish my hand
three rolls from crown to knee? No, I'm polite and
verbose. Films; drinks; the meeting goes as well
as it could, until five o'clock when he
leaves, and I wax vehement over beer
bottles. Look, baby, I *want* to be queer,
it's the light at the other end of the
long march, et cetera. Cut: a streamlined
she-torso with no feet, no hands, no head;
intercut penis/hammer; eye reads: blows:
his filmed image of—you? Woman? Who knows
(I don't) what's between you two. We spar down
slicked streets to your stop; kiss. I walk downtown.

10

The grizzled doorman lets the doctors' wives
into and out of the rainstorm. Thirty-year-
old mothers hive here till their men's careers
regroup the swarm for boxed suburban lives.
The doorman's sixty, football-shouldered, white.
The multi-racial anoraked interns
will earn, per year, at forty, more than he earns
in ten. Maybe one-tenth of the scrubbed bright
wives will earn his wages; fewer do.
Knees dovetailed at The Duchess, I'm giving you
my hours with a talk-starved woman I knew there
through her tough small girl, while on the polished square
at our boot-toes blue-jeaned women slow-dance
to a rhythmic alto plaint of ruined romance.

11

In the Public Theater lobby, I wait for Marie.
Black overcoat, brown plait: two people waltz
close, through the crowd's buzz. I watch, finding fault
with the dance's hierarchic He and She.
They weave past; Tall leads, Short follows. I see
they're women. I love them. I stand near
them, grin, wish I wore a lavender star.
Marie's here, blinking, owlish. We hug. We
go upstairs. The two women sit one row
ahead, kissing. I look at them, look away.
They are more edifying than the play
(will they laugh at woman-made misogyny?
Yes . . .) but I shouldn't stare, and when I do
I flush above the belt and throb below.

12

You're high on work, bouncing words off the ceiling
as we lie down, go down into a flurry of down,
arms and legs enlaced. My tongue around
your hillocks shudders your pleasure, feeling
its own rough touch call the blood-rush swelling
everything mutable to immanence.
We giggle at our fork-tongued eloquence,
gasp at our fingers' dazzling slide. You're telling
me about Wittgenstein and Gertrude Stein
images juxtaposed on a white wall
moving, the metaphysics of a meal
we shared, till we kiss ourselves to a wine-
drenched feast whose mute wit is a mutual
silence honed in our rapt mouths to a sign.

13

No better lost than any other woman
turned resolutely from the common pool
of our erased, emended history,
I think of water, in this book-strewn room. In
another room, my daughter, home from school,
audibly murmurs "spanking, stupid, angry
voice"—a closet drama where I am
played second-hand to unresisting doll
daughters. Mother and daughter both, I see
myself, the furious and unforgiven;
myself, the terrified and terrible;
the child punished into autonomy;
the unhealed woman hearing her own voice damn
her to the nightmares of the brooding girl.

14

And I shout at Iva, whine at you. Easily
we choose up for nuclear family,
with me the indirect, snivelling, put-upon
mother/wife, child's villain, feminist heroine,
bore. On thick white plates the failed communion
congeals. Iva bawls in her room. You're on
edge, worked out, fed up, could leave. Shakily
we stop. You wash dishes, drop one; it breaks. We
should laugh. We don't. A potted plant crashed too.
Frowning, I salvage the crushed shoots, while you
deflect my scowl with yours. You leave a phone
message for your friend, while I read one
last picture book, permit a bedtime drink
to a nude child, who's forgiven me—I think.

15

Through wet August nights we were the rev-
Olution crawling forward on each other's
bellies. Our anecdotes about our mothers
told what would be foible, what unforgiv-
able. Twenty-seven, thirty-six, five,
we three amble, howl at the March full moon
over housing projects. Iva hangs on
our elbows. "Drag me!" Our tensed arms heft live
weight, grubby and kicking. Your tired pale
face shifts in the moon-pool: a farm woman,
a raw boy, a red-lipped hedonist.
Night slims down, warms up toward our third season.
I lean above my unkempt child toward all
of them. She tugs us, "I *hate* to be kissed!"

16

Dreams play diverse cadenzas of betrayal.
I wake word-foundered. Anything I say
discovers discord. Chin to squared-off chin,
crossed arms, I worry you, "How do you feel?"
"Anxious. I feel cut off and far away."
You and I have done, will do this again:
one querulous; response: one inflexible.
I A-train uptown through the ordinary
assaults. MEN STONE FEM LIBBERS IN IRAN.
Childless, anonymous, accountable,
I gauge how wide apart to stake my knees.
Most of the faces facing me are brown.
None of the choices facing me are simple.
I can't, today, begin a sentence "We . . ."

17

I hold you, wanting whatever I want:
to taste cold water; to get up and pee;
to fuck; to know there might be space named "we"
to build on. I tend to the first two, can't
have all. You're asleep. Still in underpants,
I wash the percolator out, start coffee,
write, cross out, write more. Anxiety
shifts through the placed words' patterns, takes distance
enough that when you say my name, I lie
with you, loosened, in your waking fragrance:
soaped hair, warm bread of your skin, exhaled mint.
My eyes encounter your lacustrine eyes,
where you might, I might, miscall lust, clarity,
and I hook my tongue on something like a sentence.

18

I'll tell you what I don't want: an affair:
love, by appointment only, twice a week;
grimy, gratuitous life lived elsewhere
with others. When it's easier to speak
about than to you, when I think of you
more than I'm with you, more anxious than tender,
I feel less than a friend. There's work to do.
Artist, woman, I love you; craft and gender,
if we're antagonists, aren't in dispute.
Love starts with circumstance; it grows with care
to something self-sufficient, centered, root
from which the cultivators branch, the air
renewing them transpired rich from its pores.
Or so I hoped while I was celibate.

19

When I read poems to the art students
I wanted you there; when my ephebes, shar-
ing craft I taught, showed off, I wanted you there;
when I talk a woman around imprudence,
when I orchestrate a meeting or a meal,
when my thoughts unroll imaginal sentences,
when I come through better than I thought I was,
I want you there. But I surface seasick, feel
desire and apprehension lashed like stones
to me. Reeled toward you in the elevator,
I shrink inches from my accomplished stature
of thoughtful hero, whom you haven't seen,
diminishing to needy lover, green
with doubt and necessarily alone.

20

You separate perception from perceiver;
I make it sound like virtue that I can't.
In this imaginary argument
we've had repeatedly when we're together,
my mind is limbic, weighted like the weather.
You're sunlit on another continent.
It's rained five days here. The first two I spent
indoors, ate cheese, read magazines, neither
nourished nor informed. My anger paired
with your absence: lonely parameters.
I want to be the child-philosopher
cross-legged in the drop-leaf table's shelter;
bare legs crossed on the nubbly pile, who felt her
mind's flux find form in fixed faces of chairs.

21

Down from the hills at dawn, a thunderstorm
pounded the cabin roof. Indoors, I rolled
to the wall, a log quilted against spring cold,
and wove the noise into a ravelling dream
whose threads snapped into syllables Marie
was muttering from the upper bunk in clear
incoherence. You're not here. Iva's not here.
We sat on the porch late, in luxury
of rambling childless conversation, ate
a steak cooked on the camp stove, with Bordeaux
from New Paltz, talked more, turned in. Candlelit
again, impatient and disconsolate,
I wait afternoon rains out, rummage through
scrap thoughts while Marie writes, stalled, missing you.

22

The late-May weather's risky as a mood.
Yesterday's freighted clouds have burned away
leaving scoured sky, mud, sunlight, solitude
I frame in tin cups of thermos coffee
back on the porch with Marie. Heliotrope,
I lodge, knees up in weeds, on a gravelled slope
where tall white pines light candles for the summer.
On my knapsack strap, a V-winged bomber
modelled from a scarab perches on moon-
jitney legs, a horsefly numbed with noon
sun. I've learned to pick out a late wood-
thrush song enlacing the percussive jays.
This respite from inclement weather could
(clouds are banking up, though) last through the day.

23

As yoked to her by absence as by presence,
I image, fifteen minutes since she's gone,
her sneakers pushing leaves up as she ran
into the woods, urged on to independence
by me. Feet on the porch rail, I drink silence,
thinking: She has to cross the road alone.
If she doesn't find anyone at home
—the six-year-old gone shopping with his parents—
will she get panicky and lose her way?
Revenant, you nap. Marie drove to town.
I look up from my book, identify
the she-cardinal's sanguine rose-brown,
then check my watch. From down the path comes "Hey,
Mom!" Forty-five minutes on my own.

24

Strata of August 12: portable typewriter,
seashell ashtray, blue-and-white plastic lighter,
a jagged ochre flint from the Val d'Oise,
two amber quartz flakes, two packs of Gauloises,
tan spiral notebook, brown spiral address
book, a friend's typed essay on loneliness,
her card from Russian River, a map of France,
a blank postcard of market day in Vence,
four letters in four colored envelopes,
typing pad, cold coffee in a glass cup,
airmail envelopes in a paper band,
two felt pens, one capped, one in a beige hand,
writing, straw mat, glossy black paint that pulls
the eye on reflected light to the facing hills.

25

We work, play, don't cross-reference calendars
here. Sun gilds a scrub-oak hill; the fig tree
drops purple dry first fruit on the cement
terrace that's, for the rest of August, ours,
where you project perspectives, blond head bent
to big papers. I chart stratigraphy
of my desk, glimpse, in a pitcher, flowers
you brought, for our year, though we're both diffident
to celebrate. I start letters, can't write
what it's like, face to face, learning to live
through four A.M. eruptions, when we fight
like bruised children we were. Can I believe
persistent love demands change, not forgive-
ness, accept the hard gift of your different sight?

Index